BLOCKCHAIN AND GOVERNMENTS

SRINIVAS MAHANKALI

Sanat Bhat, Saravana kumar Malaichami

DEDICATION

We dedicate this book to all the Progressive Governments and the greatest enterprises striving to adopt Blockchain to transform our world for a secure, safer and corruption free tomorrow!

PREFACE

Onset of the Pandemic due to nCovi19 virus has heralded an unprecedented change in the mindsets of people to dramatically adopt to Technology inspired lifestyle.

Earlier, it was felt as a necessity to meet, greet and deal with people personally and engage in official and personal engagements. Now there is nothing we can think that we cannot do remotely using digital technologies.

Governments are discovering that they can dramatically improve the reach of and access to their services to citizens and businesses by embracing new technologies.

Blockchain technology along with other empowering technologies like IOT and AI & ML powered applications is facilitating a rapid disruption across every aspect of our life due to its ability to securely connect vast majority of users simultaneously. This is offering Provenance, Authenticity and Trust to transactions and reducing the cost of undertaking the business.

In this book we would like to take a design thinking approach to easily understand and adopt Blockchain with an idea to instil a 'system' based approach to this nascent field.

A number of real life casestudies in which the authors have been closely involved or have analysed threadbare have been captured in this book for easy understanding.

Acknowledgements

We are extremely thankful to the community of emerging technology professionals with whom we interact on a day to day basis during the past 3 years, working with leading companies and on great projects.

We are indebted to our teachers, senior colleagues and co-authors who have encouraged one of our authors to write a series of books on emerging technologies like Blockchain – The Untold Story, AI & ML – Agents of Automation, Secure Chains, Blockchain for Non IT Professionals and a STEM Fiction novel, Corona Wars. etc.

We would like to sincerely thank all those who inspired us and supported us in pursuing our journey in Blockchain.

We wish to thank the numerous Start-ups who toil very hard to innovate and come up with new and innovative solutions to solve the problems of the humanity and propel us forward in our evolution. We are always inspired by the Start-up world and observing them inspires me and keeps up my motivation to work hard.

PROLOGUE

Start-ups work hard to evolve new solutions that challenge the status quo and propel the world forward with new products, technologies, platforms, applications and services.

Most of the time, the inspiration to found a new venture springs out of a suffering that the promoters or their near and dear undergoes. The setbacks propel them to start a new venture and come out with a viable solution. They undergo a lot of struggles, undertake a lot of sacrifices before coming up trumps and learn to survive and thrive.

This shows that Start-ups are the masters at Identifying problems, examining options to solve problems, prioritising them and finally orchestrating a solution that scales in the long run in a viable manner.

This is also the essence of design thinking that focuses on zeroing on the customer problems that need to be solved, finally appropriate solutions that solve the problems for benefit of all use groups and stake holders.

Blockchain, one of the newest babies in the disruptive technology world, is increasingly seeing a tremendous traction of late. There is a need to come out with a systemic thinking approach to leverage this new paradigm, that seems to be having a killer potential in some domains to solve the challenges we have been facing today.

Let us delve into the design thinking approach to solve the problems using Blockchain approach.

CONTENTS

CHAPTER 1.1:BLOCKCHAIN- A PRIMER

Blockchain Technology has proved its utility beyond its original discovered use case as a unit of decentralised, distributed and Permission less crypto currency and is not being widely looked upon as a foundational technology that is disrupting a number of industries with a variety of use cases for government and enterprises. With its promise of acting as Trusted Third Party governed by automated programs driven by mathematical algorithms, Blockchain is promising to eliminate expensive non-value adding middlemen who add to a number of leakages of money and a variety of other resources that add significantly to costs. As an inter-enterprise collaborative platform, it is promising to take economies of scale to a totally different scale, benefiting the entire participating eco-system.

The technology has the potential to significantly benefit the humanity by dramatically lowering costs and improving trust in transactions through built in transparency aided by almost immutable & tamper-evident transactions.

In this chapter, we shall look at Blockchain Technology fundamentals and a variety of prominent use cases across different domain, in different countries and also look at a number of Consortiums implementing Blockchain solutions.

ORIGIN & EVOLUTION OF Blockchain & How it all started.

Bitcoin protocol that was launched on January 3rd,

2009, the first known application of the Blockchain technology paradigm, reliably provided a solution for achieving such a consensus in distributed systems that create and transact value over the internet without fear of 'Double-spending.'

This problem was formulated into a story called 'Byzantine General's Problem' where a group of nine generals decided to attack a fort they were surrounding, subject to the majority's decision despite being handicapped by improper communication facilities. A 25-year wait after the problem's formulation, Bitcoin successfully demonstrated a solution for the computer systems to achieve Byzantine tolerance even in face of a sizable number of adversaries and adverse conditions.

There are different types of consensus mechanisms like POW (Proof-of-Work), POS (Proof of Stake), DPOS (Delegated Proof of Stake), PoET (Proof of Elapsed time), PBFT (Proof of Byzantine Tolerance), RBFT, RAFT, N2N and many more.

A detailed discussion on these various consensus mechanisms is out of the scope of this manuscript and several white papers are available for understanding and evaluating the same.

Bitcoin, the first implementation of the Blockchain paradigm:

Blockchain technology was demonstrated successfully through its first use case, 'Bitcoin.' Bitcoin Blockchain is a living example to show that

this often doubted and misunderstood technology is a new paradigm that has come to stay with us for a very long term. Bitcoin is the first implementation of Blockchain technology consisting of six primary elements:

a. An updated Distributed ledger replicated across all the peers undertaking transactions through the platform, consisting of the updated status of Unspent Outputs (UTXO) in chronological order.
b. A network of nodes undertaking to verify and propagate the transactions generated by the participants.

c. A group of miners dispersed across the world to mine the transactions to ensure the authenticity of the same, maintaining the integrity of the Blockchain for all times to come, using an automated execution of the protocol defined by the consensus algorithm called 'Proof-of Work.' 'Proof-of-Work' represents the amount of work that the miners undertake by utilizing their computing power and electricity spent, to be eligible for block rewards in the form of newly mined coins as per a predefined formula.

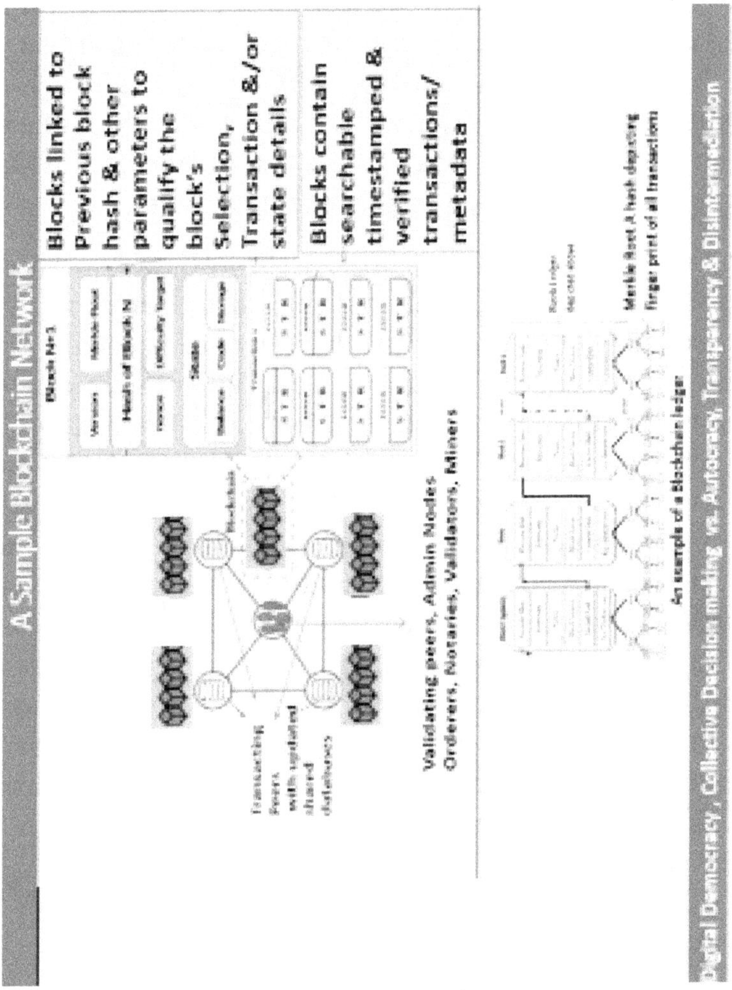

Fig 1.1 Sample Blockchain Network.

d. Blockchain wallets used by the participants to initiate transactions and store the value in the form of UTXOs or unspent transaction outputs measured in the number of Bitcoins.

e. The value that is exchanged across the platform, namely the 'Bitcoin' or its fraction, which is treated as a cryptocurrency with all the properties that we associate

with the fiat currency in the real world, except the unitized physical representation and regulatory approvals.
f. Exchanges that facilitate buying and selling of cryptocurrencies and derived products known as tokens among themselves using wallets and conversion of the same into fiat currencies in a dynamic manner.

Bitcoin has proved that billions of dollars' worth of value can be exchanged across the world from one person to another unknown person, without the need of a trusted central party, a bank or Government in this case. As on 1st February 2021, over 18 million Bitcoins with an approximate total value of over 500 billion US Dollar at a unit price of over 30000 US Dollars are in circulation. The success of Bitcoin led to the launch of several variations of alternate Blockchains for a variety of purposes. The majority of them are cryptocurrencies with different properties in terms of privacy, speed of execution, consensus mechanism for transaction validation, the most prominent variation was proposed in the form of the Ethereum Blockchain platform by Vitalik Buterin and his team at Ethereum foundation which we shall discuss a little later.

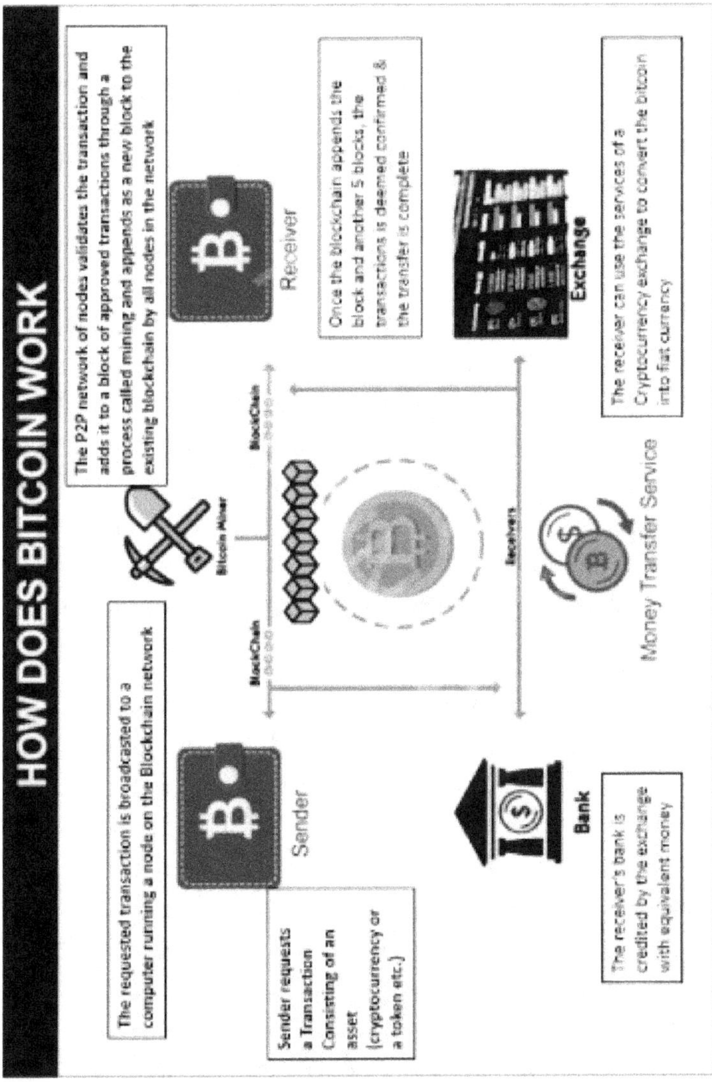

Fig 1.2 How Does Bitcoin Work.

Over the years, the cost of infrastructure in the form of storage space and processing power required for IT applications has come down substantially. The availability of high-quality Cloud service providers has reduced the

need for investments in high cost on premise infrastructure. Approaches like 'Open-source technologies, decentralized methodologies' and 'Pay-as-you-go-for-services consumed' are combining to facilitate the employment of cutting-edge technology powered infrastructure to find new solutions to
our problems, rather cheaply. Messaging Protocols, Event-driven communication and record updation, API (Application Programming Interfaces) are facilitating collaboration between applications across multiple on-Premise and Cloud-based applications acting together seamlessly. IBM, Microsoft, Oracle, Amazon and many leading organizations are offering high-end secure IT applications including Blockchain as a service that can facilitate the large-scale implementation of automation enabling technologies in a convenient and cost-effective manner.

What is Blockchain?

Blockchain is an augmented Peer to Peer Distributed Ledger Technology employing advanced cryptography to secure identities of participants in the network undertaking timestamped, immutable transactions with decentralised processing to exchange data & change ownership of assets using cutting edge technology powered applications also known as Smart contracts running inside the system providing Transparency, Security, Tamper resistance, Auditability and enhanced Trust through system acting as Trusted-Third-Party in Triple-entry accounting as shown in the following figure.

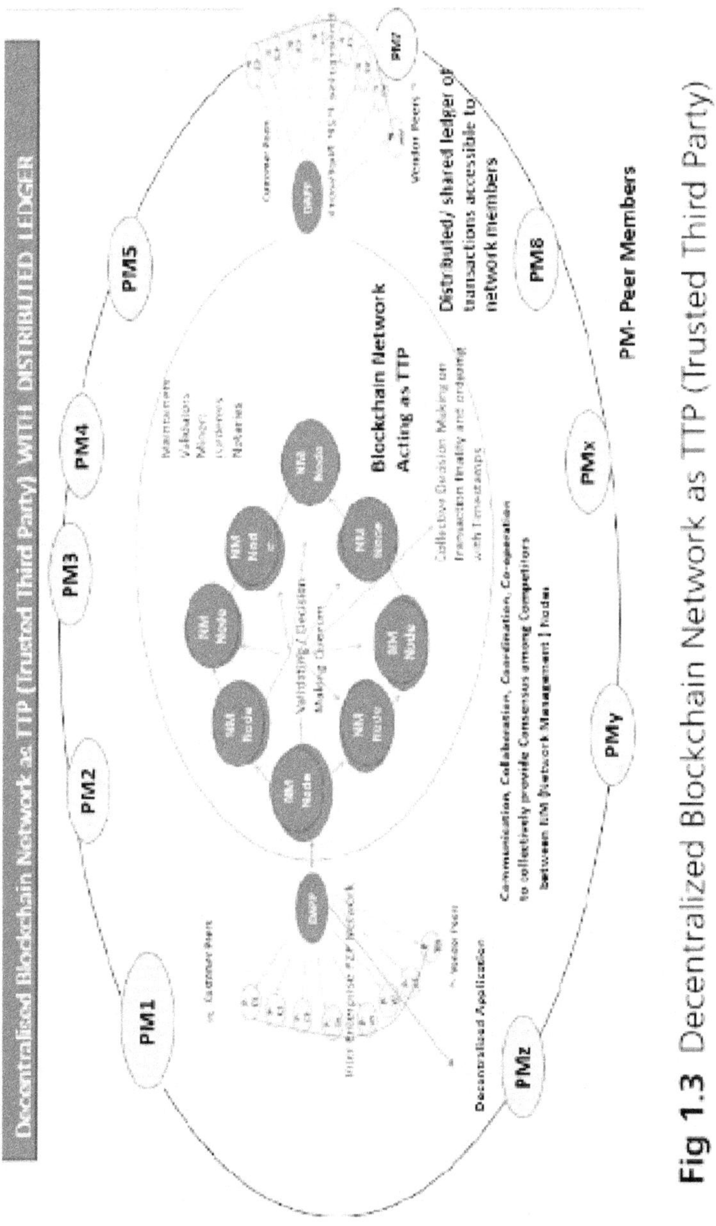

Fig 1.3: Blockchain as a Trusted-Third Party in Triple entry account-

ing

BLOCKCHAIN: AN AUGMENTED DISTRIBUTED LEDGER TECHNOLOGY:

Blockchain is a Distributed Ledger that uses peer to peer consensus within a Decentralized Network to validate transactions and a hashing algorithm to cryptographically link them in a Chronological chain of records.

1. Copies of ledger are shared across computers known as 'Nodes in the network'
2. Computerised record of historical transactions chronologically ordered.
3. Shares resources directly between nodes bypassing third part network with specialized communication protocols.
4. Every transaction must be approved (or rejected) by Consensus mechanisms (Ex: POW, POA, POS, DPOS, PBFT, RBFT, Raft etc.)
5. Hosted by many nodes simultaneously controlled by no single entity. Data is accessible by anyone within the network.
6. Public Permissionless networks like Bitcoin & Ethereum, Permissioned networks like Hyperledger, R3 Corda, Quorum
7. Transactions may include moving currency, updating a standard enterprise records, transferring ownership of an asset etc.
8. Converting transaction data to a fixed length string of numbers and letters that cannot be reverse engineered (ex: SHA 256).
9. The hashing process of a new block includes meta data from the previous block's hash

output. The link makes the chain immutable.

10. A full immutable time-ordered history of transactions approved by the network.

RESILIENT DATA STRUCTURES OF BLOCKCHAIN:

We have seen that in the traditional approach, the participants in a typical business scenario pretty much operate in silos and all the parties are connected to the centralized big marketplace or the dominant player who connects the buyers and sellers or provides the services to the clients globally.

Instead, Blockchain presents an inter-enterprise scenario that offers a 'Single Source of Truth' where all the peers are connected to every other peer with a possibility to conduct peer-to-peer transactions as per business logic codified in the form of Smart Contracts. Even the dominant player, though while being the facilitator could still be a player whose returns depend on the quantity and quality of the business dealings happening on the network.

The Single Point of Failure has always been the bane of most of the centralized organizations which maintain their databases under a single command, control and administration. This is the weakness most often exploited by the Ransomware virus creators who were behind some of the most lethal attacks on global organizations by unleashing the WannaCry virus.

While distribution and shared database also help in non-repudiation by the parties undertaking transaction, the ability to reconstruct the database from other members of the network eliminates the risk of the SPOF from this very route, thus blunting the weapons of the cybercriminals. This minimizes the risk by tilting the RRR (Risk-

Reward-Ratio) away from the investors of these crooked instruments.

Thus, Blockchain is seen as the vehicle for safe and secure automation at scale.

Traditionally we are used to centralised databases for storing data which respect the CRUD methods for manipulating data, namely Create, Update, Update and Delete. We also come across replicated data bases under the command and control of the same IT Administrator's control. Blockchain, a programmable database differs from the traditional databases in a number of ways, as captured in the following figure.

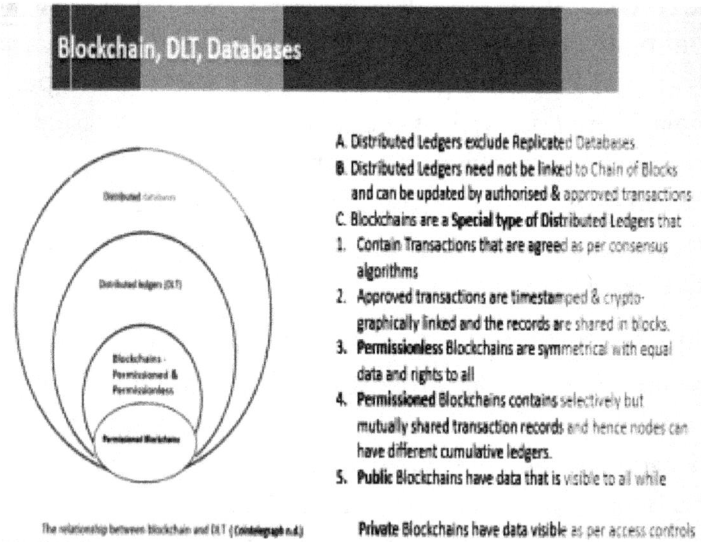

Fig 1.4: Blockchain & its connection with Databases & Distributed Ledger Tech.

As seen in the above diagram, Blockchains can be classified as follows:

i. Permissioned – If the membership and the validator pool is restricted and must be approved by an admin authority like in the case of Hyperledger Fabric, R3 Corda,

Quorum etc. In a Permissioned Blockchain, ability to conduct transactions or write data is restricted as per access control rights

ii. Permissionless – If the membership and the validator pool is not controlled and accessible with equal opportunity to anyone like in the case of public Bitcoin and Ethereum platforms.

In case the data stored on the Blockchain is accessible for viewing to anyone without restrictions, then it is considered a **Public Blockchain** and if the access is strictly restricted and is kept confidential to a selected group of participants, then it is considered **Private Blockchain.**

If a Blockchain is set up and implemented by a dominant player who controls the access and validation, it is termed Private Permissioned and in case a group of participants work together then it is termed a **Consortium Blockchain or Federated Blockchain**.
In general, Blockchain databases can be considered SALT databases as per the context may be. In the context of Permissioned Blockchain systems, SALT may be described as Sequenced (timestamped), Agreed (decided in a manner agreeable to the participants as per an approved program), Ledgered (maintained in a database of key-value pairs reflecting the state of ownership of assets and Tamper resistant (almost impossible to change the order of the records committed).

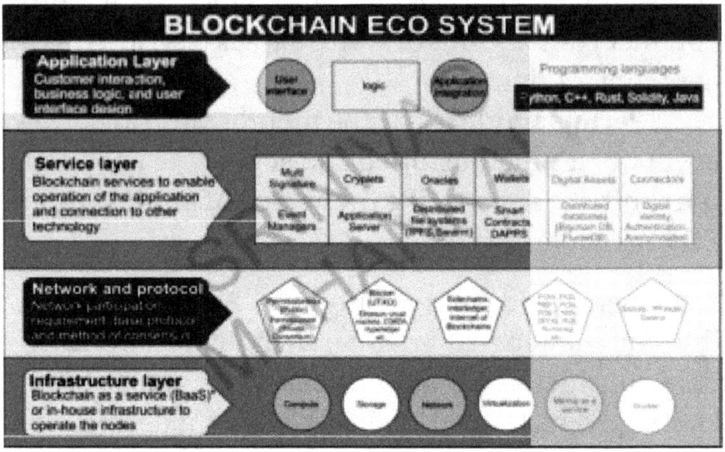

Fig 1.5: An integrated representation of Components of Blockchain eco-system

COMPONENTS OF BLOCKCHAIN

A typical Blockchain application cuts across 4 key layer as depicted in the earlier figure.

When a building is constructed it consists of 5 key levels of infrastructure as follows:

1. Land area on which it is built. This depicts the infrastructure layer.
2. The foundation of the building and the pillars that form the scaffolding of the building from the Technology layer that comprises of the Network and protocol. There is a lot of science that goes behind this layer.
3. The applications that automate the processes that are re-engineered to simulate the workflows are a part of the smart contract based decentralised applications, This represents the architecture of the building and is more a work of art.
4. The user interface of the application is similar to the design elements that allow the inhabitants of the building to move in and with necessary safeguarding to ward off intruders and allow insiders.

Thus, this analogy can be represented as in the following diagram that depicts the various layers, activities and the actors involved in building solutions for a typical Police Department in Government, based on Blockchain application.

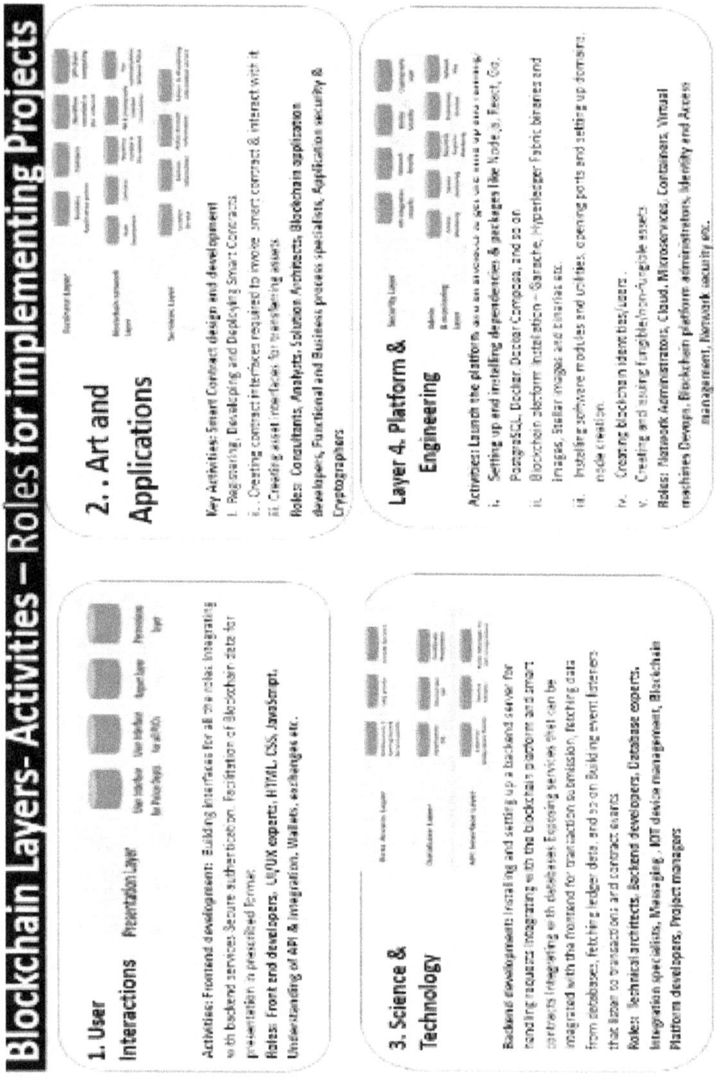

Fig 1.5-2: Layers, activities and Actors in a Blockchain Business

Blockchain Combines Encryption, Encoding, Hashing, PKI, Timestamps, DSA and Broadcast for the Internet of Value by bringing Privacy, Permission, Password management within the reach of an individual peer and frees him/her from the dependence on the Trust Anchors who have now grown unduly large leading to a centralized internet Blockchain converts the traditional internet infrastructure as we know through its TCP/IP protocol from the Internet of Information to the Internet of Value, by acting as a Trusted Third Party to any peer to peer interactions. The features of Blockchain that facilitate this are shown in the following figure.

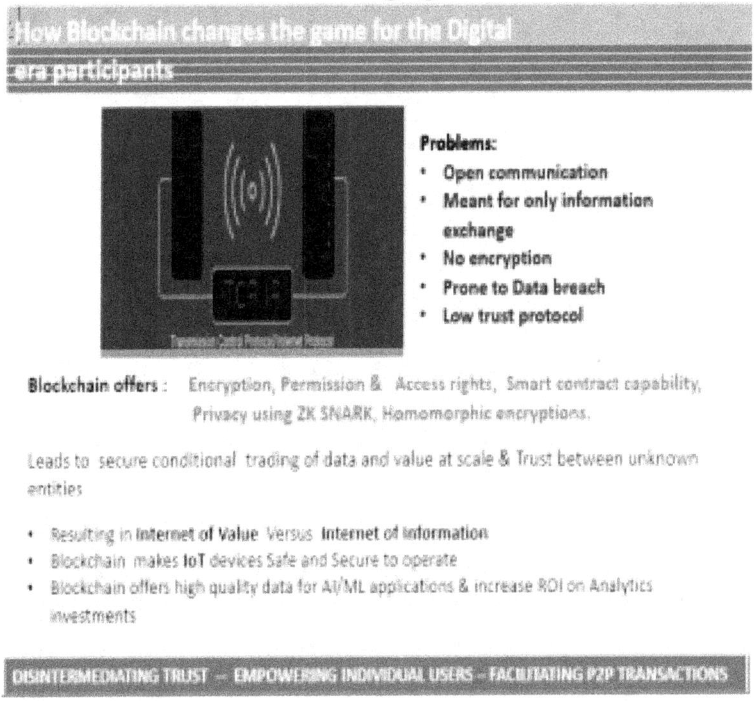

Fig 1.6: How Blockchain changes the game for the Digital Era Participants

Blockchain combines the cryptographic and programmatic paradigms like encryption, encoding and hashing in a unique manner to achieve amazing benefits offering a new paradigm of trusted disintermediated transactions.

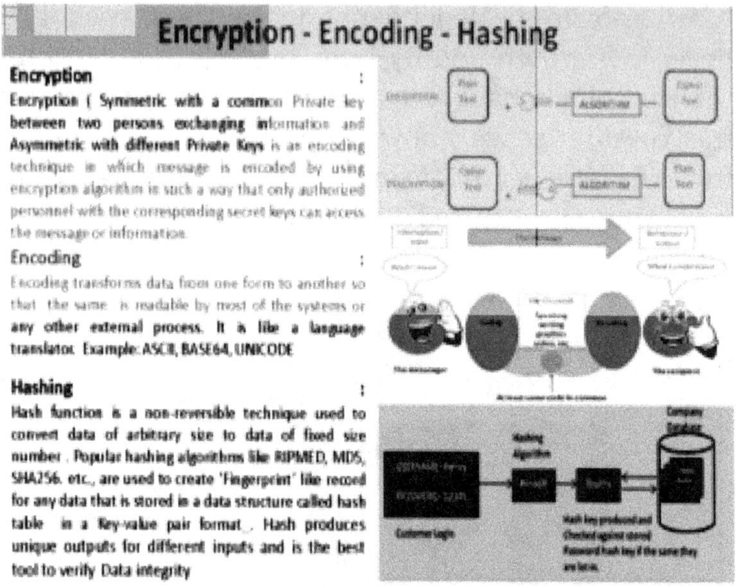

Fig 1.7: Encryption – Encoding – Hashing

i. Hash function: A hash function produces a unique fixed length output for a corresponding input of any size (like a thumb impression of a human being), which cannot be replicated. Hash of any information is treated as the unique and indisputable representation of the information. Hashes form the heart of Blockchain as the blocks are represented by the hash of the information and are chained together as a linked list of chronologically mined and validated blocks.

ii. Merkle root (Root of roots): While a hash is a unique number derived out of the base number, the Merkle root is derived from hashing pairs of transactions together until only one element is
left. Since the hash was unique, a change in any transaction would result in a change in the Merkle root, which would be easily caught.

iii. Public-Key Infrastructure: To facilitate secure electronic transmission of information and undertake ultra-safe transactions, Blockchain employs several cryptographic applications. PKI or Public-Key Infrastructure is a set of technological procedures used to create, manage, distribute, use, store, and revoke digital certificates. PKI is used to authenticate participating parties using public keys and corresponding private keys connected to each other through complex algorithmic relations, requiring rigorous proofs to confirm identities for facilitating information exchange. PKI uses X.509 certificates to identify the owners of public keys.

a. **Private key and Public-Key:** The Private Key and Public-Key pair is (Private key being the secret password and Public key being the corresponding username known to all) used to encrypt information using mathematical algorithms, rendering decryption virtually impossible without these keys. Computationally, it is similar to the factoring of prime numbers, which is a simple, mathematical procedure. However, decomposing the result is difficult without prior knowledge of its factors.

b. **RSA:** PKI systems normally use RSA algorithms for linking public keys and private keys. RSA (Revest–Shamir–Adleman) is one of the first public-key cryptosystems and is widely used for secure data transmission. In such a cryptosystem, the encryption key is public and it is different from the decryption key which is kept secret (private).

c. **ECDSA:** Blockchain systems use Elliptical curve cryptography to issue secure Public-key Private key pairs. The messages are encrypted by a digital signature algorithm namely, ECDSA that ensures that only authorized owners of targeted messages can securely decrypt the messages.

iv. Digital Signatures: Digital signatures are a unique aspect of Blockchain transactions and provide a layer of security to carry out and validate genuine transactions. A digital signature is a mathematical scheme to present the authenticity of digital messages or documents. A valid digital signature gives the recipient reason to believe that the message was created by a known sender (authenticated by verifying against the public key of the sender), and the sender cannot deny having sent the message (non-repudiation by signing with his/her unique Private key), or that the message was not altered in transit.

v. X.509 Certificates: In Permissioned Blockchains like R3 Corda or Hyperledger Fabric, the participating members are provided X.509 certificates by the administration Certificate authority for identification by the network. An X. 509 certificate is a digital certificate that uses the widely accepted international X. 509 public key infrastructure (PKI) standard to verify that a public key belongs to the user, computer or service identity contained within the certificate.

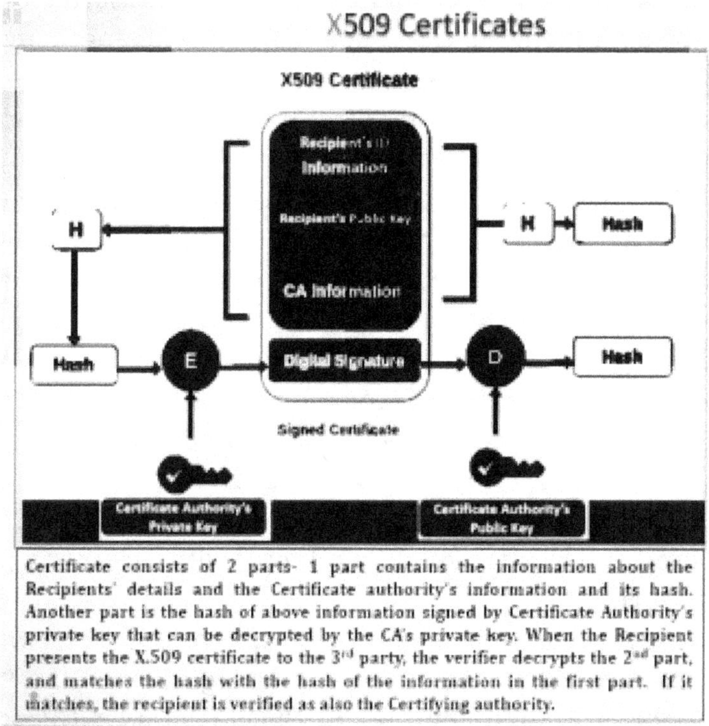

Fig 1.8: X.509 Certificates for certifying identities in permissioned scenarios

vi. Consensus Mechanisms (POW, POS, DPOS, PBFT, etc.): The mechanism by which members come to an agreement about the authenticity of a transaction is referred to as the 'Consensus Mechanism.' Consensus formation ensures the involvement of multiple validators in a systematic and predetermined manner, ensuring decentralization and objectivity of decision making. It ensures implementation of the key features of the Blockchain platform like increased trust, immutability of the transactions, and maintenance of the integrity of the platform. The consensus mechanism is the soul of the Blockchain platform and has to help members in reaching the right decision all the time. The sanctity of the Blockchain application depends on the strength and reliability of the consensus mechanism. The consensus mechanism followed by Bitcoin and the earlier version of the public Ethereum client is known as 'Proof-of-Work (POW)' where miners or validators compete with each other and burn valuable resources like computing power and enormous amounts of electricity to guess the right Nonce (number used only once) and create a targeted hash to win the race to create a block. Proof-of-Work —followed by Bitcoin Blockchain and some versions of Ethereum Blockchain—consumes a huge amount of resources to arrive at a deterministic consensus. The Ethereum platform will soon shift to a 'Proof of Stake' based consensus, which involves negligible energy consumption.

Some new-generation public platforms use variations of 'POW' and 'POS'-based consensus algorithms like PoET (Proof of Elapsed Time) and DPOS (Delegated Proof of Stake) to minimize resource utilization and wastage. Enterprise Blockchains use energy-efficient algorithms like 'Proof of Authority' (POA), Practical Byzantine Fault-Tolerant' (PBFT), 'Node to Node' (N2N) and their variations to arrive at a deterministic consensus.

As it can be seen, the discovery of the Blockchain paradigm has been achieved by an ingenious combination of the various simple tools and techniques that have been in vogue for decades. Let us now define Blockchain with our understanding of the various components, features and benefits offered by this unique technology.

Thus, many permutations & combinations are possible depending on the ability to read, write or vote on the transactions.

In the case of Governments, we come across ***Public Permissioned Blockchains*** which are restricted for writing and maintaining, but the data could be accessed by all the citizens for verification like in the case of certain type of certificates or ownership records.

The important feature of this Blockchain approach is the 'decentralized' approach where the decision regarding the correctness of the transactions is taken without recourse to an individual entity's authority and muscle power. The transactions with due approvals and authorizations representing the real-life scenario are sent to a pool of network managers, who can then collectively follow a designated approach and vote on the transactions to be included in the approved chain of events that influence the records and ledgers permanently.

The decentralized pool of miners is referred differently in different Blockchain systems and serves to increase the uptime of the network manifold while minimizing the risk associated with a centralized approach. While in Permissionless Blockchains we have mining pools or set of validators, on Permissioned Blockchains for enterprise applications, they operate as a set of Orderers (Hyperledger Fabric), Notaries (R3 Corda), Validators (Hyperledger Sawtooth, Indy) and the like.

CHAPTER 1.2: BLOCKCHAIN PLATFORMS FOR REAL LIFE APPLICATIONS

Ethereum which was launched after Bitcoin with improvisations, allowed businesses to create decentralized versions of real-life applications that we see in the day-to-day world through the implementation of 'Smart Contracts' which are programs created to replicate the business agreements into applications that can be run on Blockchain databases.

A **"smart contract"** is simply a piece of code that is running on Ethereum. It is called a "contract" because code that runs on Ethereum can control valuable things like ETH (ether – native crypto currency on Ethereum Public network) or other digital assets. Smart. Contracts abstract real-life business agreements into applications on a decentralised network of computers running
Ethereum nodes in the context of EVM (Ethereum Virtual Machine). The EVM runs as a local instance on every Ethereum node, but because all instances of the EVM operate on the same initial state and produce the same final state, the system as a whole operates as a single "world computer."
EVM is considered Turing complete which means it can solve any reasonable complex computational problem.
One technically implements logic in say Python and translate to Solidity the Smart contract programming language to implement sophisticated logic. In the case of Permissionless Blockchains like Ethereum, the transactions forwarded by clients are validated by a pool of miners who win the opportunity to create a block of valid transactions that is then appended to the Blockchain, eventually updated by all the nodes of the plat-

form.

Thus, the approved transaction becomes a part of everyone's ledger thus becoming immutable and tamper resistant.

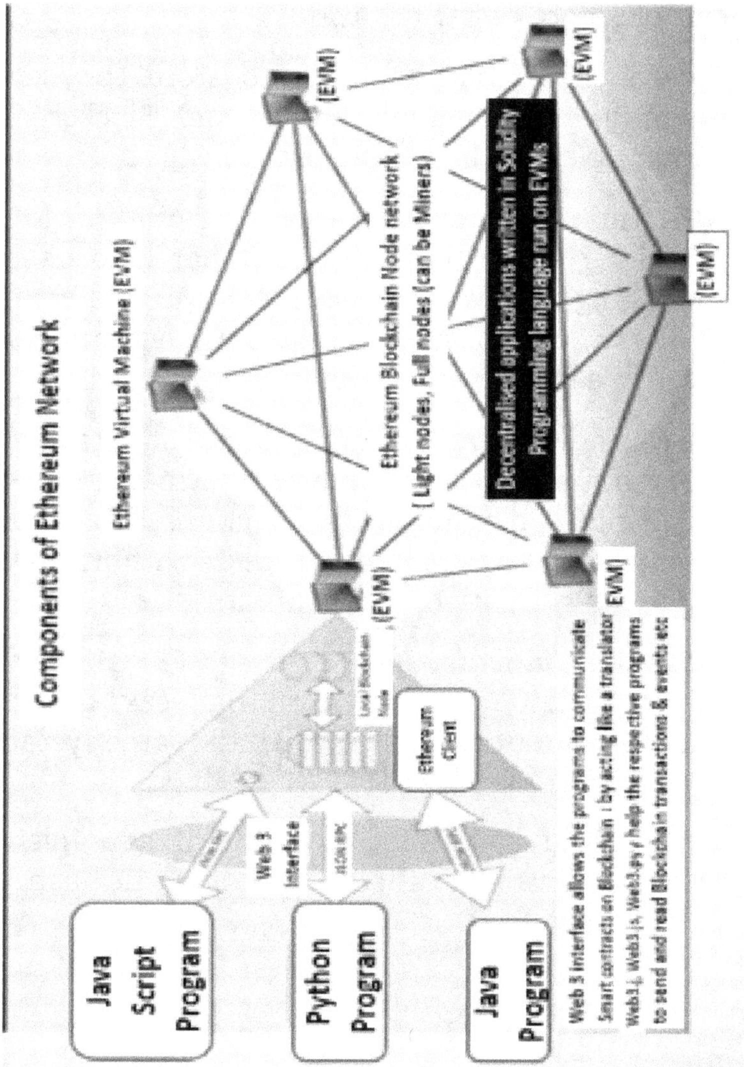

Fig 2.1 Components of Ethereum Permissionless Network

There are various client software that have been created for this platform. It does not have high data storage capabilities. Storing and retrieval of complex data have limitations.

To overcome this, we need to store the data off chain and manage them through Blockchain compatible data bases and technologies.

IPFS (Inter planetary File server -https://ipfs.io/) and Swarm are two protocols that help us in managing large amounts of data off the chain in a way, referenceable across the Ethereum network in a decentralized manner.

We can now address large amounts of data with IPFS, and place the immutable, permanent IPFS links into a blockchain transaction. This timestamps and secures your content, without having to put the data on the chain itself.

The Inter Planetary File System (IPFS) is a peer-to-peer distributed file system that seeks to connect all computing devices with the same system of files. In some ways, IPFS.

Each file and the blocks within it are given a unique fingerprint called a cryptographic hash.

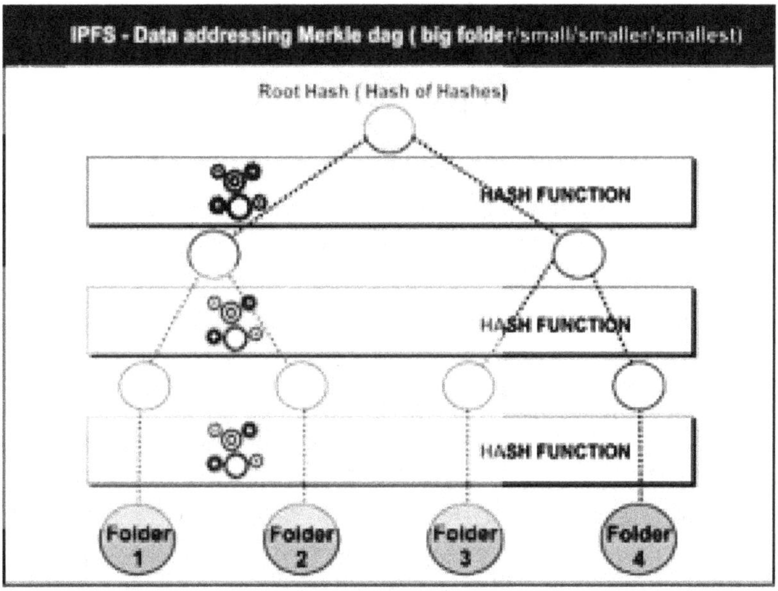

Fig 2.2. : IPFS leveraging Merkle tree data structures

When looking up files, you're asking the network to find nodes storing the content behind a unique hash. By inserting the hash of the data pointing to the file on the nodes, instead of large files through the Smart contract, we can dramatically enhance the capability of the Blockchain platform at a very nominal cost.

HOW DO THE FILES LOCATED IN IPFS IN THE CONTRACT OWNER'S COMPUTER INTERACT WITH THE ETHEREUM NETWORK?

The developer of the smart contract will allow the files of its users to be stored in IPFS enabled system. The metadata of the files are stored across all the nodes in the blockchain. When a user queries for the metadata, the blockchain returns the corresponding files required by querying the same by referencing the corresponding IPFS hash link embedded in the smart contract.

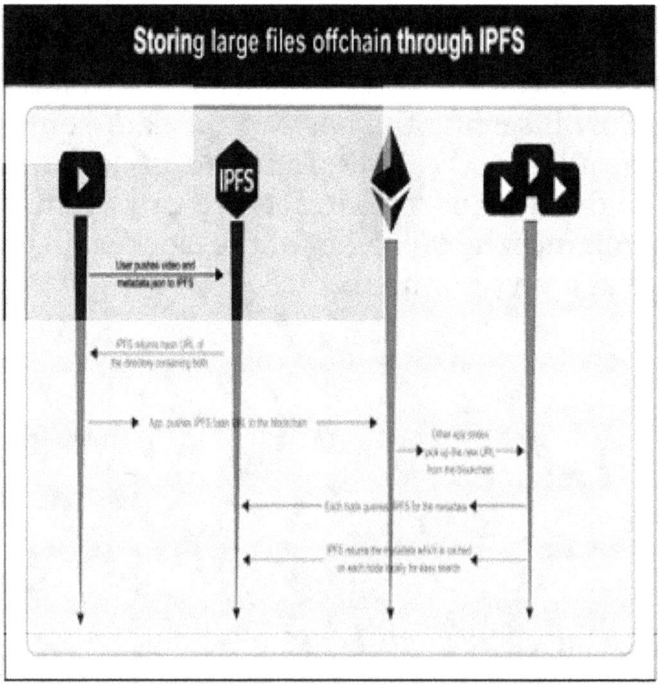

Fig 2.3. : Storing Off-chain Files using IPFS

The user will interface with Blockchain through a web interface, interacting with the Blockchain through an API.

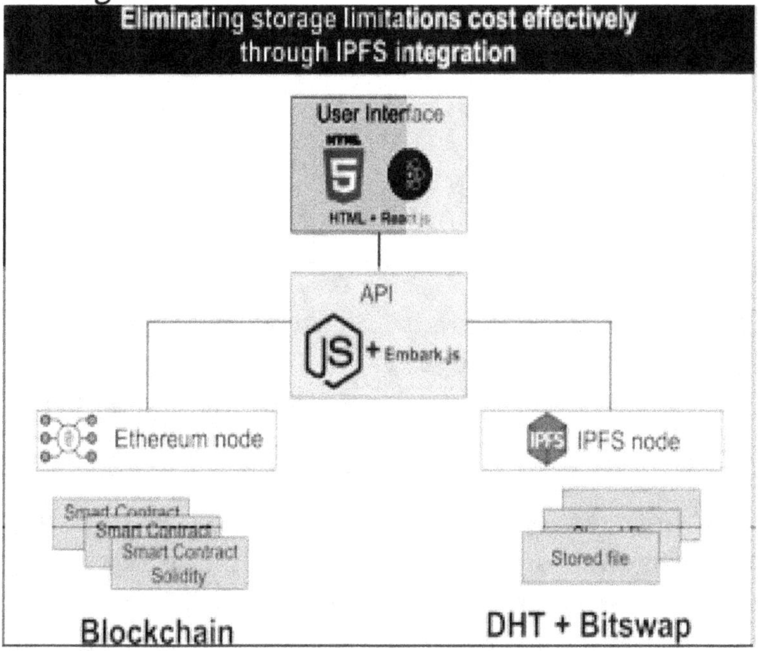

Fig 2.4. : IPFS integration for storing large volumes of off chain data referenced on Blockchain by hash.

Ethereum also supports SWARM, a decentralized file system platform similar to IPFS, which comes integrated with the Blockchain platform to manage large files off its main chain. While it is similar to IPFS in many ways, transactions involving storing files in Swarm need to be paid in Ether thus increasing the cost of participation marginally. (https://github.com/ethersphere/swarm)

> Swarm is a distributed storage platform and content distribution service. It is a native base layer service of the Ethereum web 3 stacks. The primary objective of Swarm is to provide a sufficiently decentralized and redundant store of Ethereum's public record, in particular to store and distribute Dapp code and data as well as block chain data. From an economic point of view, it allows participants to efficiently pool their storage and bandwidth resources to provide the aforementioned services to all participants.
>
> From the end user's perspective, Swarm is not that different from WWW, except that uploads are not to a specific server. The objective is peer-to-peer storage and providing a solution that is DDOS-resistant with zero-downtime, fault-tolerant and censorship-resistant as well as self-sustaining. Self-sustenance is achieved by a built-in incentive system which uses peer to peer accounting and allows trading resources for payment. Swarm is designed to deeply integrate with the devp2p multiprotocol network layer of Ethereum as well as with the Ethereum blockchain for domain name resolution, service payments and content availability insurance.

Enterprise Blockchain platforms like Hyperledger Fabric, Quorum, etc., were developed as variations of the Ethereum platform while enterprise applications like Multichain and R3 Corda took inspiration from the architecture and other elements of Bitcoin Blockchain.

Hyperledger Fabric works on the concept of Channel,

which is a private network within the quorum of all the nodes on the system, that share a business logic and are parties to transactions as per an approved smart contract also called a Chain code. The data is shared amongst the participants as per access control and privacy requirements to maintain confidentiality unlike in the case of Ethereum which broadcasts the information on the ledger to all the participants. Transaction flow in typical enterprise Blockchains like Hyperledger Fabric is described in the following figure:

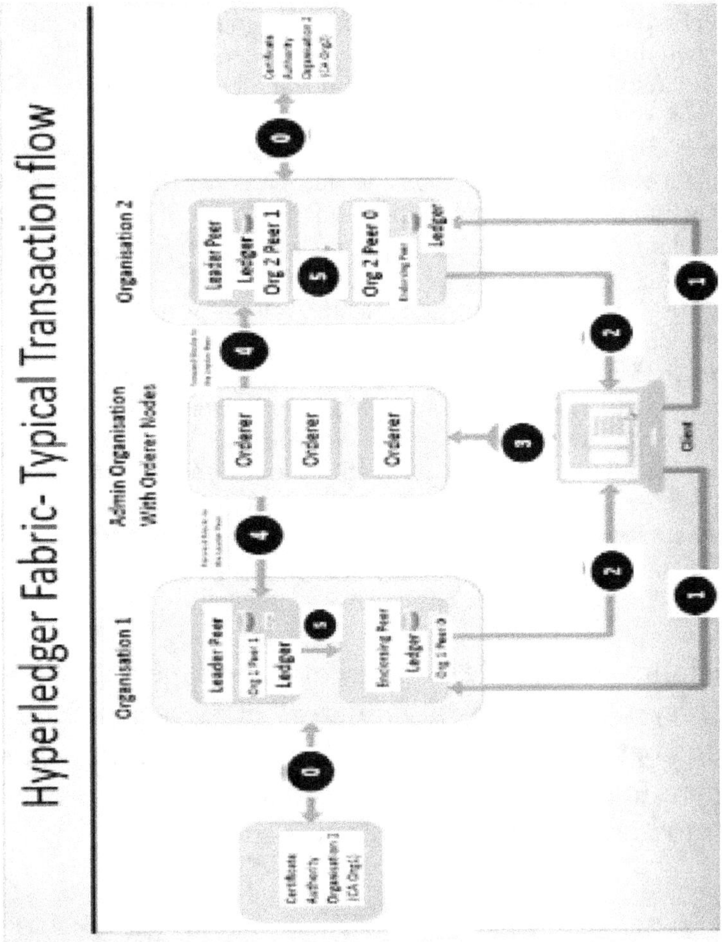

Fig 2.5 – A typical transaction flow in a Permissioned Blockchain Hyperledger Fabric Network's Channel

The step-by-step process in a Hyperledger Fabric channel for initiating a transaction from a peer to the time it is committed on the ledger are as follows:

Step 0: The Certificate authorities in the respective organisations provide the cryptographic identities to the respective peers and the same information is disseminated to all the other counterparties involved in transactions with the respective peers.

Step 1: Client sends Transaction Proposal to Endorsing peers (who must approve as per Business logic encoded in the channel's Chaincode).

Step 2: Endorsing peers attest the transaction and send back to Client with their digital signatures

Step 3: Clients sends the fully approved transactions along with the endorsers' signatures to Orderer.

Step 4: Orderer verifies the transaction's validity and includes the same in a block along with the time stamp. As per the block interval/ block size limit encoded, Orderer creates a block of valid transactions and sends the read/write sets to respective organisation's Leader Peers.

Step 5: Leader Peer distributes the blocks to all the peers in the organisation who are the channel members

Step 6: The validating peers upon receipt of the blocks, update their respective ledgers with valid approved transactions consistent with their current state.

Step 7: Transactions not consistent with the current state of the respective member ledgers are nullified but continue to be a part of the Blockchain ledger.

Distributed Ledger Platforms like R3 Corda do not work on the concept of Blockchain.

They follow the Triple entry accounting concept, where a Notary node acts as a validator to guarantee transactions between counterparties, as per pre-configured business logic. Notary checks and ensures the validity of the transaction and prevents double spend.

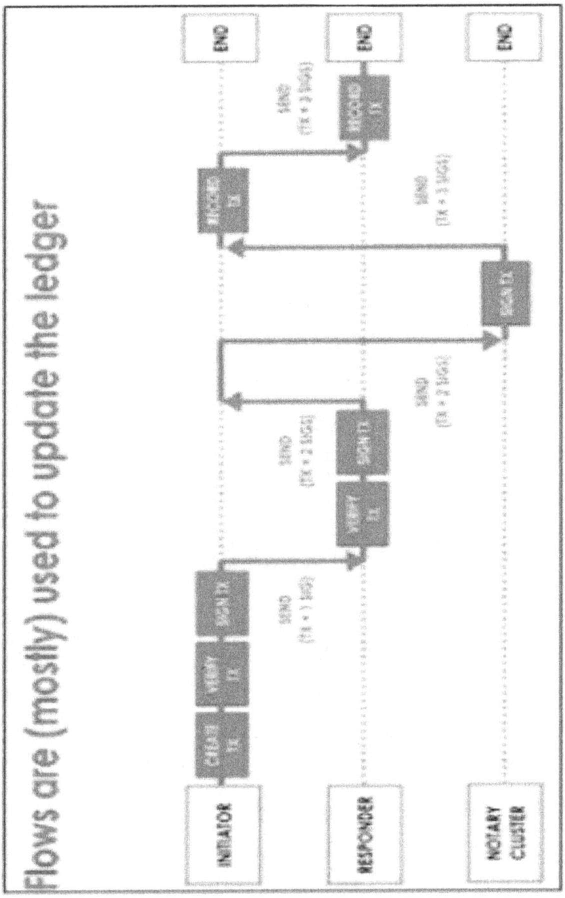

Fig 2.6. : Corda Transaction flows updating the Ledger

STELLAR:

Stellar is an open-source protocol for exchanging money backed by Non-profit Stellar foundation.

Stellar allows for transfer of value across the world over internet through servers that run software implementation of the protocol, forming a global value exchange network. Each server stores a record of all "accounts" on the network in a "ledger". The transactions submitted through the clients are approving as per a consensus protocol and the ledgers are synchronised every 3-4 seconds.

Stellar offers Smart contract functionality with applications written in JavaScript, Java and Go. It uses a proprietary consensus mechanism SCP that is a significant improvement over Proof of Work that result in no cost of mining and high throughput of 1000 transactions per second with an average block time of 3.5 seconds.

Stellar is ideally suited for financial transactions that involve transfer of money across countries. Non-profit and microfinance companies use Stellar to move funds across the word.

Crowd funding through ICO linked to its currency, XLM is one of the prominent use cases of stellar protocol.

In 2018, Stellar announced their affiliation with Key base to eliminate the need of extended cryptographic addresses for international transactions.

NEM:

Malaysia based NEM, uses a cryptocurrency XEM as a native token. It uses a unique Consensus mechanism called POI (Proof of importance) that gives weightage to the miners in proportion to the number of tokens held in conjunction with the average duration of holding. Their miners who hold over 10000 tokens have a chance of earning additional rewards.

NEM is built from scratch as a powerful and streamlined platform for application developers of all kinds, not just as a digital currency. Using NEM in your application is as simple as making RESTful JSON API calls allowing you to configure your own "Smart Assets" and make use of NEM's powerful blockchain platform as you are fast, secure and scalable solution.

Configured for your use, NEM is suitable for an amazing variety of solution classes, such as direct public transactions via streamlined smartphone app, efficient cloud services that connect client or web applications.

NEM offers an enterprise version useful for extensive enterprise level use cases with secure functionality like, Digital identity, Crowd funding, Token launch through ICOs, Educational records management system etc.

NEM offers additional security for users through

multi-signature wallet implementation.

NEM smart contracts can be coded in Java. NEM offers customized templates that ease the task of development of smart contracts.

NEO:

Neo is a China based Public Blockchain platform that offers a number of advantages over Ethereum.

Neo claims to combine the power of Blockchain technology and uniquely created high security identities of users to create smart assets than can be operated upon by Smart contracts for a new generation of transactional activities.

Digital assets are programmable assets that exist in the form of electronic data. The use of blockchain technology to realize asset digitization has features such as decentralization, mediation, trust less, traceability, and high transparency. NEO supports multiple digital assets at the bottom level. Users can register assets on NEO, freely trade and transfer, and resolve the mapping relationship with physical assets through digital identities. The assets registered by users through a compliant digital identity are protected by law.
Digital identity refers to the identity information of individuals, organizations, and things that exist in the form of electronic data. The current mature digital identity system is based on the PKI's X.509 standard. In NEO, we will implement a set of X.509-compliant digital identity standards. This set of digital identity standards, in addition to the X.509-compliant hierarchical cer-

tificate issuance model, will also support the Web of Trust peer-to-peer certificate issuance model.

The biggest feature of the NeoContract smart contract system is the seamless integration with the existing developer ecosystem. Developers can use C#, Java, and other mainstream programming languages to develop, debug, and compile smart contracts in familiar IDE environments (Visual Studio, Eclipse, etc.) without learning a new programming language.

NEO's universal lightweight virtual machine NeoVM is highly deterministic, highly concurrent, and highly scalable. The NeoContract smart contract system enables millions of developers worldwide to quickly develop smart contracts. NeoContract will have a separate white paper describing the implementation details.

CARDANO (ADA):

Originally known as the Ethereum of Japan, ADA offers a number of versatile features to its platform adaptors. Founded by an Ethereum developer, Charles Hoskinson, ADA is supposed to possess advanced quantum resistant features against malware attacks. The Blockchain platform offers smart contract functionality as well as a strong Digital identity system of regulatory standards.

Smart contracts on Cardano are programmed in Haskell and it uses Aurobro's Proof of stake consensus algorithm with a high resistance or DDOS attacks due to higher transaction fees with no remuneration for mining.

Using an approach known as side chains, Cardano SL, a general-purpose cryptocurrency enables domain specific cryptocurrencies, such as Ethereum Classic. This way, any innovation developed via domain specific cryptocurrency can have participants who hold value in a general-purpose cryptocurrency. Examples of such applications are identity management, gaming and gambling, and verifiable computations. The unique feature of Cardano is its wallet which allows interoperability between a variety of cryptocurrencies and in future aims to offer interoperability with fiat currencies making it easy for any entrepreneur in the world to launch their DAO even if the cryptocurrency is not allowed in their region by the respective governments.

There are many more such platforms and new age platforms incorporate advanced & customized consensus and privacy standards & follow zero knowledge proof-based protocols while also addressing the concerns of scalability, high throughput, interoperability an integration. The whitepapers and concept papers on the respective topics need to be kept in sight on a dynamic basis.

BLOCKCHAIN AS A SERVICE- VARIOUS PLATFORMS AVAILABLE

Setting and Scaling up a Private Blockchain:

Microsoft, IBM, Oracle, Amazon and Huawei are offering cloud based services to set up and scale the Blockchain applications in a seamless manner

The following are the prerequisites for any Blockchain as a Service application:

1. Scalability
2. High Availability
3. Disaster recovery
4. Secure access and Key management services
5. Single sign-on to a variety of integrated applications
6. Ability to conduct private transactions over secure channels in a confidential manner.

Blockchain as a Service offering from global leaders like Microsoft, IBM, Amazon, Oracle and Huawei offers dependable, scalable and secure platforms with all these features.

HUAWEI: BLOCKCHAIN AS A SERVICE (BCS):

https://static.huaweicloud.com/upload/files/pdf/20180416/20180416142450_6
1761.pdf

Leveraging its strengths in Mobile and Telecommunications, Hardware
technologies, Cloud, Connected cars, IoT and cutting edge security technologies, Huawei is offering an end to end integrated blockchain development, deployment and maintenance services encompassing activities like

- Planning
- Purchasing
- Configuring
- Development
- Product Launch
- Operation and Maintenance of Blockchain technology for organizations.

Based on Hyperledger Fabric platform, Huawei offers versatile features like secured & encrypted peer to peer network with high level of security for all account and transactions, pluggable consensus algorithms, smart contract functionality and secured cloud services to clients for applications in IoT, Supply chain, Financial Services and auditing, connected cars, Identity verification, telecom carriers, cloud network, tokenization of assets and securities etc. This will enable clients across the world to leverage the power of blockchain technology and also be in tune with the advancements across all the cutting-edge technologies, without being overawed by the same.

IBM LinuxONE Blockchain Services
(www.ibm.com/LinuxONE/Blockchain)

Based on Hyperledger platform, IBM offers production ready blockchain platform to easily build, manage, scale and govern Blockchain applications.

- IBM LinuxONE Blockchain assures 99.999% uptime,
- End to end encryption for all data
- Transactions with security of highest-level commercial security classification.
- Scale up to 30 billion queries in a day
- 170 dedicated cores with 8000 Virtual machines and 32 Tera bytes of memory.
- Reduced development time and speedy activation and management of ongoing management of the entire business network with a variety of collaborative tools.

IBM has over 400 in production Blockchain instances across Supply chain, Finance, Healthcare, Pharma, Education, IOT industries and for Government applications reflecting its immense experience, stability and dependability of its platforms.

Amazon BAAS (https://aws.amazon.com/blogs/aws/get-started-with-blockchain-using-the- new-aws-blockchain-templates/)

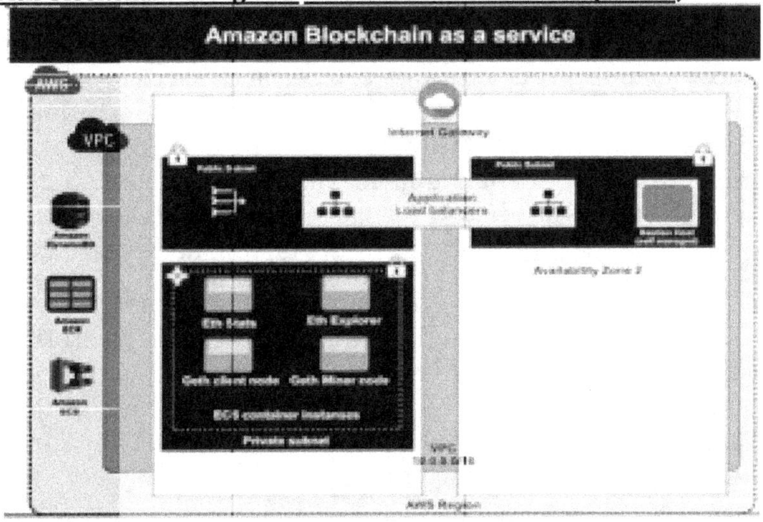

Fig 2.7: Amazon Blockchain as a Service

In collaboration with Digital Services Group, Amazon offers Blockchain services on the cloud. Amazon offers Hyperledger and Ethereum platforms on a pay as you go basis. It offers open source platforms for easy and instant deployment of smart contract applications with permissions and access controls for peer to peer transactions with distributed consensus algorithms.

Microsoft Azure BAAS (https://azure.microsoft.com/en-in/solutions/blockchain/)

Microsoft offers secure, scalable and versatile Blockchain as a service platform to rapidly develop and deploy secure Blockchain applications that are interoperable across all the enterprise applications like CRM, Big Data, Analytics, Project management, Social media and the like.

Microsoft in collaboration with Blockapps offers a comprehensive Platform to develop application on

Ethereum enterprise platform using STRATO client.

STRATO is the best way to build apps on Ethereum. Our client, written in Haskell, provides a highly scalable Ethereum compliant blockchain with an industry standard RESTful API. Blockapps provides the fastest development platform for building and deploying Ethereum blockchain applications. Our quick deployments and RESTful API enable developers to build, test and deploy smart contracts faster than ever.

With Azure BAAS, clients can pay & scale as they go. Depending on a trusted Cloud provider, they can run their applications from anywhere in the world. In collaboration with Alpha Point, Microsoft offers Digital Asset exchanges to facilitate enterprises to store, track and trace digital assets.

In collaboration with IOTA Tangle, Microsoft offers a variety of solutions the IoT and Microfinance Industries.

IOTA Tangle is a DAG (Direct Acrylic Graph) based distributed ledger that offers an absolute light weight CORE that will enable applications to run on Micros sensors, very much needed by IoT devices. IOTA offers huge scalability with a unique consensus schema that will enable more transactions to be handled as the number of participants' increases, with zero mining fees.

IOTA's architecture allows setting up a settlement and transactional network for IOT clusters and a built-in transfer layer allowing easy coupling of streams of compensation. With IOTA, Microsoft enables clients to set up one click payment channels for IOT devices, Oracle connectivity to collect and connect live external data as required, and also develop ultra-fast and versatile side chains. To set up a Blockapps STRATO virtual instance of a Blockchain platform in a few minutes, please visit https://developers.blockapps.net/install/azure/.

Azure Blockchain Development Kit (https://github.com/Azure-Samples/blockchain/tree/master/blockchain-development-kit)

The **Azure Blockchain Development Kit** is built on Microsoft's serverless technologies and seamlessly integrates blockchain with the best of Microsoft and third-party SaaS.

This kit extends the capabilities of our blockchain developer templates and **Azure Blockchain Workbench**, which incorporates Azure services for key management, off-chain identity and data, monitoring, and messaging APIs into a reference architecture that can be used to rapidly build blockchain-based applications.

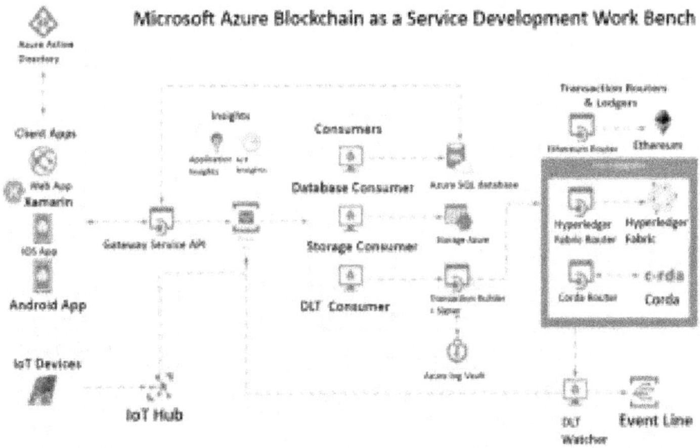

Fig 2.8 Azure BAAS Development kit

Azure BAAS Development Workbench provides a rich developer scaffold to develop and integrate blockchain solutions within an enterprise. It simplifies Blockchain application development by providing a solution using several components. It can be deployed using a solution template in the Azure Marketplace. The template allows us to pick modules and components including Blockchain stack, type of client application and support for IoT integration. Once deployed, Blockchain workbench provides access to a web app, IOS app and Android App.

These tools have become the first step for many organizations on their journey to re-invent the way they do business. Apps have been built for everything from democratizing supply chain financing in Nigeria to securing the food supply in the UK, but as patterns emerged across use cases, our teams identified new ways for Microsoft to help developers go farther, faster.

This initial release prioritizes capabilities related to three key themes: connecting interfaces, integrating data and systems, and deploying smart contracts and blockchain networks.

Oracle BAAS:

https://cloud.oracle.com/en_US/blockchain :

Oracle offers enterprise blockchain applications

on Hyperledger Fabric platform to enable clients to:

- Provision blockchain networks
- Join other organizations
- Deploy and run smart contracts to update and query ledger

- Conduct trusted transactions with suppliers & banks
- While integrating seamlessly with existing new cloud based or on-premise applications.

Oracle BAAS enables organization to expand enterprise boundary through trusted dependable, enterprise grade managed platform as a service in a speedy manner to:

- Create trusted networks
- Automate with smart contracts
- Develop and Integrate applications
- Conduct Private transactions
- Rapidly add on new members
- Administer and Monitor networks through an easy-to-use user interface.

Leveraging its strengths in enterprise applications, database technologies, ERP solution and experience in open-source technologies, Oracle stands to make rapid strides in the Blockchainification of organizations as a major enabler.

CHAPTER 2:

Types of Problems Blockchain can solve

Blockchain offers a readymade inter-enterprise platform that abstracts several complexities that would otherwise be very complex and tedious IT applications to create between multiple non-trusting parties to interact with each other.

By mediating in an automated fashion between non-trusting parties it allows competitors to collaborate and cooperate in a coordinated manner through seamless communication over a distributed system. It offers varying degrees of centralisation depending on the type of governing council that could range from a centralised body like Government that empowers a number of other connected and regulatory body members to authorise & facilitate transactions on one end and on the other, to a completely decentralised administration like in the case of Public permissionless Blockchain platform like Bitcoin, Ethereum and the like.

The Trusted Third-party approach facilitated by the Blockchain is captured in the following figure.

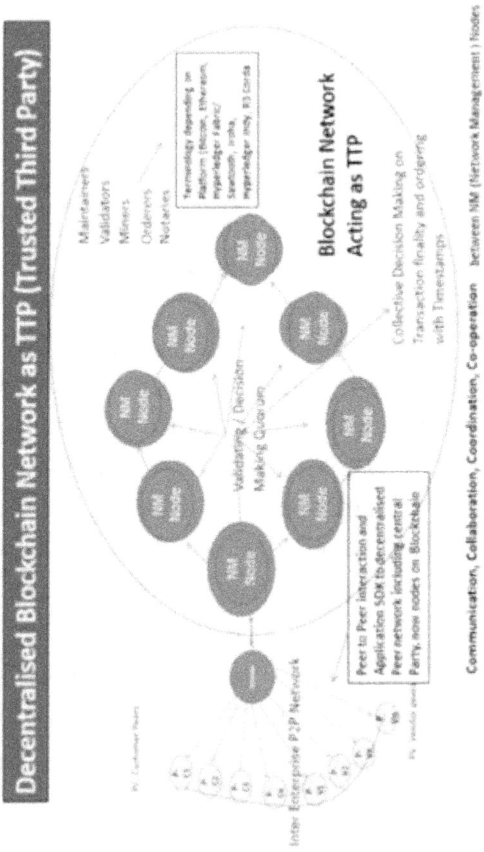

Fig 2.1: Blockchain as Decentralised Trusted Third Party among transacting participants

It can be observed that the most difficult aspect of implementing Blockchain projects is to get different parties to agree upon a common approach to solving problems collaboratively.

The projects initially start with a single ownership and very few nodes and after successful conclusion of the Proof of concept of the benefits, tend to scale up fast into multiple nodes with an increased participation amongst the eco-system players. The challenges to governance dramatically increase even as the benefits increase dramatically due to network effect due to economies of scale.

What are the returns for the Blockchain infrastructure provider?

The users of the platform have a lot to gain in the form of increased efficiencies, better services provided to their customers and a drastic reduction in third party risk, increased cybersecurity and resilience and reduction in operational costs owing to digitization. For this, they will pay a fee to the administrating organization of the Blockchain platform as per an agreed pay-per-usage model thus resulting in a win-win scenario.

In the case of Permissionless Blockchains like Bitcoin and Ethereum, heavy costs are incurred by the maintainers of the consensus mechanism who offer the TTP benefits to the participants. For this, the miners are rewarded by a combination of currency minted by the network and the transaction fees paid by the participants.

While in the case of Enterprise Blockchains the participants' identities are fully disclosed and verified for compliance with the regulatory authorities, in the case of Permissionless Blockchains, there is a real possibility of ill-intentioned and malicious participants to take over the network or push illegal transactions leading to 'Double-spending.'

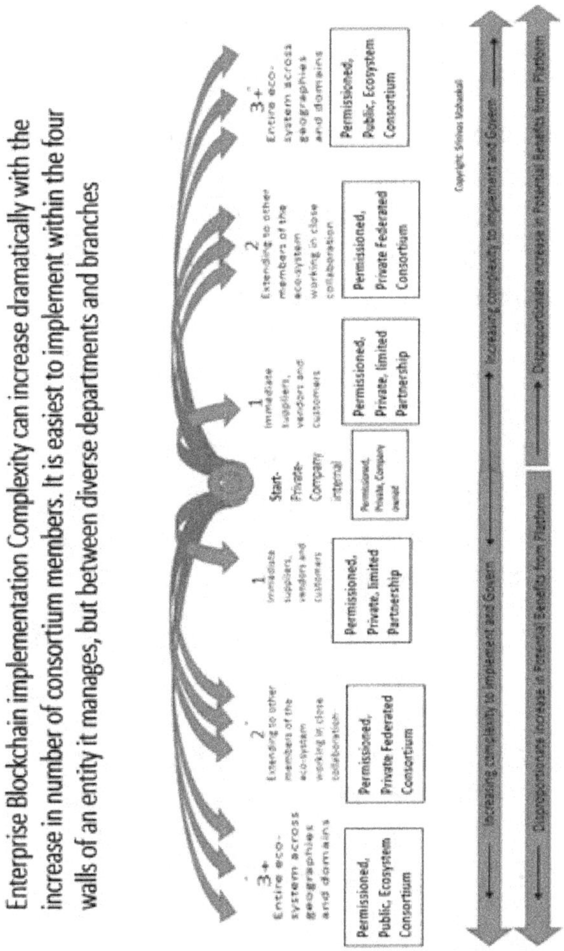

Fig 2.2: Blockchain Platform Benefits versus Complexity

This is a routine issue with smaller sized Permissionless platforms, in the case of large platforms like Bitcoin and Ethereum, the network pushes the miners to spend a high amount of resources like computer processing power and electricity to validate their transactions. This leads to a negative ROI (Return on Investment) for

malicious participants making it non-remunerative to attack the system. However, the fall-out of this is that the Permissionless Blockchain platforms consume disproportionately high resources that could one day pose a threat to environmental sustainability.
There is an increasing tendency to innovate on different types of resource-efficient consensus algorithms for use by Permissionless Blockchain platforms (example: DPOS, Tendermint, Proof of Stake, Proof of Elapsed Time, etc.), which could be explored in detail by technically minded professionals.

Some of the key applications for Blockchain that can dramatically improve the quality of governance and facilitate trust, transparency an increase citizen satisfaction are summarised below:

1. Durable Record keeping - Example: Health records, Educational records, Municipal Records.
2. Chain of Custody- Provenance, Authenticity, Trust based Track and Trace- Example, Pharma, food, Land records, Bonds etc.
3. Multiple Agency Collaboration- Example: Income tax, Market places , Auctions, Procurement, Project Management.
4. Trusted high value Transactions – Example: Insurance, Letter of credit, Benefit distribution, Loan disbursement.
5. Increase transparency –Evidence recording, Certificate & License issues, Identity verification.
6. Eliminate middlemen to save time & cost– Example: Market place, Cross Border currency transfer

7. Cyber Security- Example: IoT, Autonomous cars, Drones through whitelisted registry-based communication

Fundamental to all this is a Proven Digital Identity and KYC management system that is authentic, fool-proof with secure verification management system that assures privacy of individual citizens, authorities, devices or applications.

The approaches to implementing Blockchain applications are described in the following chapters.

CHAPTER 3: DESIGN THINKING IN PERSPECTIVE

Design thinking is the process of empathising with the potential, existing and targeted customers to innovatively solve the problems and create products and solutions for the internal and external stakeholders. Design thinking refers to the cognitive, strategic and practical processes by which design concepts (proposals for products, buildings, machines, communications, etc.) are developed.

A 3 staged five-phase description of the design innovation process is described by Plattner, Meinel, and Leifer as:

Stage 1: Inspiration behind the project and understanding the problem: This understanding can be documented in a brief which includes constraints that gives the project team a framework from which to begin, benchmarks by which they can measure progress, and a set of objectives to be realized.

1. (Re)Defining the problem & Hypothesis- The business or the entrepreneur is inspired to solve a compelling problem that presents an opportunity for significant improvement in the status quo. In this stage, the identified problems are formulated into a hypothesis that points towards suggested solution, from the customer perspective.

2. Need finding and Design Challenge formulation from Customers‘ perspective: The customers’ needs and wants are crystallised and converted into Design challenges.

The problems that the customers face are converted

into design challenges by comparing with ideal scenarios and comparable situations that point out to solutions being in place.

Designers approach users with the goal of understanding their wants and needs, what might make their life easier and more enjoyable and how technology can be useful for them. Empathic design transcends physical ergonomics to include understanding the psychological and emotional needs of people—the way they do things, why and how they think and feel about the world, and what is meaningful to them.

Stage 2: Designing and Validating the Solution:

3. Ideating (Divergent and Convergent thinking):

Ideation is idea generation. The process is characterized by the alternation of divergent and convergent thinking, typical of design thinking process.

Divergent thinking, involves diverse groups of stakeholders in a structured brainstorming process of "thinking outside the box."

Convergent thinking, on the other hand, aims for zooming and focusing on the different proposals to select the best choice, which permits continuation of the design thinking process to achieve the final goals.

4. Building: Best ideas generated during ideation are turned into concrete products or services. These are then prototyped and are then tested, evaluated, iterated, and refined. A prototype, or even a rough mock-up helps to gather feedback and improve the idea. Prototypes can speed up the process of innovation because they allow quick identification of strengths and weaknesses of proposed solutions and can prompt new ideas.

The Prototype process generally consists of 2 steps:

i) Low fidelity prototype or a Proof of Concept where

the solution is demonstrated in a controlled atmosphere without much interaction with the existing systems and with nominal investment.

ii) High Fidelity prototype or Pilot Project: The successful and improvised low fidelity prototypes are then passed onto the next stage that involves a lot of time, effort, involvement and investment of management time. These are subjected to the real-life scenarios and are observed for the impact and expected improvements without any adverse effect.

5. Testing. The process repeats itself by looping back through inspiration, ideation, and implementation more than once as the team refines its ideas and explores new directions.

Stage 3: Impact assessment and maintenance:

Assessing the impact and finetuning the process by revisiting the earlier steps for continuous improvement.

Design thinking offers an interesting process and a set of tools that simplifies the process of finding solutions to complex problems and to design interesting solutions, products and services for entrepreneurs and corporate leaders.

Blockchain being a disruptive & new paradigm extensively leans on design thinking approach to evolve and implement the solutions for complex problems.

CHAPTER 4: APPLYING DESIGN THINKING TO BLOCKCHAIN

Blockchain defined as an Augmented Distributed Ledger Technology is very much valuable for streamlining inter-enterprise processes and by employing a new generation of applications known as Smart contracts, facilitates collaboration, coordination and collaboration through real-time communication between unknown peers across the world for trusted, secure and transparent transactions.

Being an inter-enterprise platform, it is not amenable for a variety of applications that are internal to the organization.

It is very imperative to put in place a common agenda for several ecosystem players and ensure that the 'Why Blockchain' and 'What is in it for me' part of the questions are convincingly put forth and demonstrated.

Gartner, a leading Technology & Management research advisory & consultancy in the world has outlined a three-phase approach to implementing Blockchain solutions across five different dimensions. The dimensions outlined by Gartner to describe a true Blockchain system are distribution, encryption, immutability, Tokenization and Decentralization.

Distribution implies sharing the ledger of transaction records across multiple parties of the system, across globe.

Decentralization implies a collective decision-making and ensures no single person or entity control over the decisions and assets in the Blockchain system.

Immutability implies that the transactions cannot be reversed once approved and recorded on the ledger,
Encryption helps in secured access and authorization to participants for conducting transactions and authorization of transactions to ensure the intended parties as per access protocols recorded in the system are followed by using PKI based approaches, ECDSA algorithms to link public keys and private keys and usage of hashing for preserving data integrity, ZKP protocols for privacy protection, etc.
Tokenization results in the digitized representation of real-life assets, rights and identities on the Blockchain for tracking them through their lifetime.
The three Phases of implementation are described below:
Phase-1: Blockchain-inspired solutions: These solutions involving a few but not all of the five elements described above are incremental in nature, mostly supplementing the existing business processes without causing any disruption or distraction. These are mostly centred around the creation of Proof of Concepts and Pilots to establish Proof of value and achieve incremental benefits for increased efficiencies and improvement of existing processes.
Phase-2: Blockchain-complete solutions: Once the enterprises are confident about the value proposition of Blockchain applications, a gradual expansion of scope to complement existing processes, replace them with inter-enterprise collaborated processes for greater economies of scale and tremendous benefits to their customers will be implemented. During this phase, the scope also involves leveraging all the five elements mentioned earlier.

Phase-3: Enhanced-Blockchain solutions: Involves combining different emerging technologies like Artificial intelligence, Machine learning, Internet of things with all the five elements of the Blockchain for integrated applications for autonomous agents, smart cities, supply chains, etc., for secured scaling and accelerated disruption.

Investments in Blockchain become viable when the size of the network increases and grows bigger and bigger so that the investments are amortized over a larger value of businesses generating increased savings.

Deciding on Blockchain Implementation:

But before the need for Blockchain as a solution is decided upon, it is imperative to consider all other options to solve the problem in hand through traditional approaches. The following figure gives a list of questions that need to be answered, leading to the decision to implement Blockchain as a solution to solve the problems and provide a high Return-On-Investments.

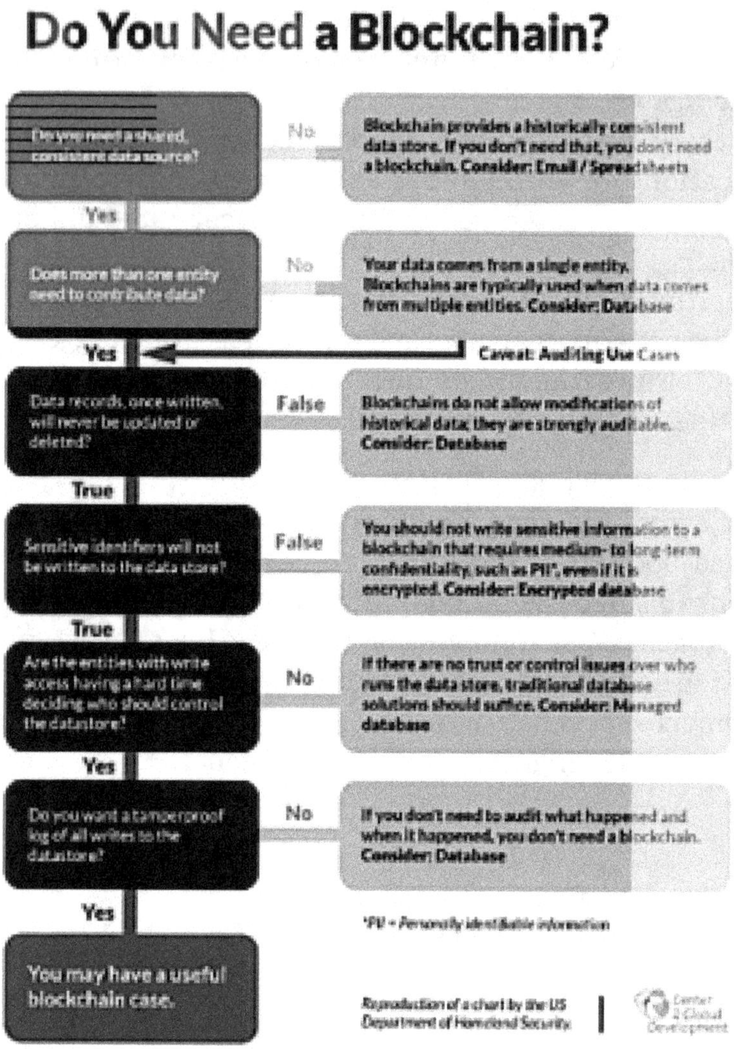

Fig 4.1 Do you need Blockchain?

While the existing incumbents involved in running the businesses across the Governments are comfortable with the centralized approaches, the choice of a decentralized approach and Distributed Ledger Technology for the future is seen as a decision that may yield substan-

tial returns but are fraught with unforeseen risks. As the technology is still in its early stage of adoption, several factors need to be considered by the decision-makers to undertake the decision to migrate to the new paradigm. The following table gives a bird's eye view of the aspects to be considered for evaluating the suitability of a Distributed Ledger Technology-based solution.
Source:https://www.cgdev.org/publication/reassessing-expectations-Blockchain-and-development-cost-complexity A high-powered committee with the involvement of the top management professionals should consider and analyze the various aspects of the problems to be tacked and evaluate the potential solutions.

Implementing Blockchain

Design Thinking, the process of evolving customer focused solutions is an interesting tool that is very much applicable to conceptualisation, implementation of Blockchain applications.

World has been using a number of approaches to problem solving and solution development. Some of these approaches are compared in the following figure.

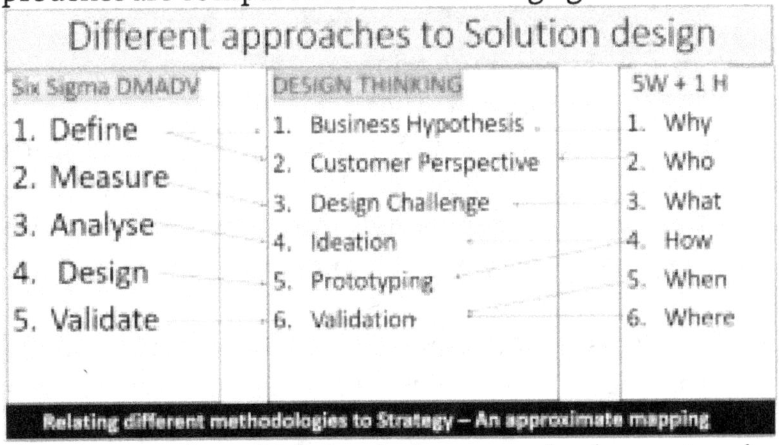

Different approaches to Solution design
Six Sigma DMADV
1. Define
2. Measure
3. Analyse
4. Design
5. Validate
DESIGN THINKING
1. Business Hypothesis
2. Customer Perspective
3. Design Challenge
4. Ideation
5. Prototyping
6. Validation
5W + 1 H
1. Why
2. Who
3. What
4. How
5. When
6. Where
Relating different methodologies to Strategy – An approximate mapping

Fig 4.2: Comparison of Solution design approaches in an enterprise context

The Six Sigma Perspective:
A six-sigma-based approach with the following steps is the most appropriate way forward for a disruptive and new-generation technology like Blockchain.
The steps are outlined as follows:
1. Define: Identify and clearly outline the problem in hand to be solved.
Mapping the stake holders: All the stakeholders like Internal stakeholders, external stakeholders, individual, organisational and even application / IoT stakeholders, that are being addressed for solving the problems need to be outlined well in advance and mapped to ensure that their interests are protected, problems solved and their value enhanced.
For example, if we are designing a Project management platform for Infrastructure projects, some of the stakeholders could be:

- Real Estate Developers
- Architects and Engineers
- Design Consultants
- Main and Sub Contractors
- Specialist Contractors
- Suppliers/Vendors
- Statutory Authorities

Problems faced by the different stake holders need to be considered and addressed. In the application, there could be access modules developed for each of these stakeholders to carry out the roles assigned to them respectively.
Phase 2. Measure: Measure the key performance indicators that need to be impacted and evaluated for improvement and provide a measure for the Return on Investment. Benchmark with the best practices and other

related/alternative solutions for assessing potential benefits.

Phase 3: Analyze: Analyze various options, potential solutions and available platforms to arrive at the best-case option by considering all possible parameters like investments required, resources and all implementation-related challenges.

Phase 4. Design: Architect the solution from various angles like data flows, entity relationships, information management, application development and technological and infrastructural considerations. Security considerations for the applications and all associated environments have to be thoroughly thought through and factored in.

The design has to thoroughly take into account various aspects like confidentiality, interoperability, confidentiality and privacy requirements, cybersecurity issues at various levels and the issues relating to compatibility with existing legacy systems and integration thereof.

As the existing centralized systems offer high transaction throughputs, the trade-off of the transaction volumes and speed with respect to the benefits like overall process-related gains, in the long run, need to be considered and factored in the design.

Seamless integration with the legacy systems, payment gateways and banking systems, ability to board new members, new processes and also drop them if required should be an important design element so that the assets and identities can conduct transactions across multiple platforms with ease through APIs or other appropriate middleware.

Phase 5. Validate: Undertake a two-stage approach of implementing a POC (Proof of Concept) for demonstrating the effectiveness of the solution without impacting the organizational systems, in case of an untested application without time-tested use case scenarios and then undertaking a pilot project by integrating the solutions in a limited and isolated environment.

Once all implementation-related issues are thoroughly evaluated, problems taken care and benefits validated, it is then time to scale up the solution to encompass a multi-department & multi-enterprise scenario.

Blockchain being a new technology paradigm, there is not much information available on the Return-on-Investments, though intuitively, most of the time it is very clear at the outset that the process excellence and the exponential benefits due to ecosystem collaboration are very much evident to the initiators with long-term vision.

When a Blockchain platform is created, all the applications possible between the participants on the same network can be envisioned and the returns quantified to evaluate the commercial viability with respect to the investments required.

From the service provider's point of view, Performance contracting that rewards the platform providers and the IT partners with a combination of fixed and savings-dependent variable revenue model can help get the Blockchain projects kicked off the ground in a win-win manner.

Example of a Blockchain platform designed & developed to solve the problems of Project Management in Infrastructure Industry:

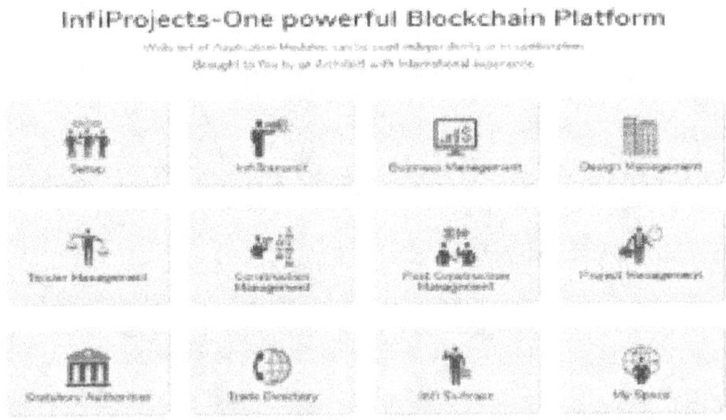

Fig 4.3: A Blockchain Platform for managing Infrastructure Projects

InfiProjects consists of several convenient modules suited to the infrastructure industry ranging from Design Management, Construction Management to Handover. User has flexibility to use any or all modules.

1. A cloud-based platform operating on a SaaS model.
2. User can sign up and establish his credentials
3. Competitive payment plans and flexibility to top up anytime.
4. No limitation on the number of projects, stake holders or transmittals.

In the module InfiTransmit, the user can:

- setup roles and permissions,
- create projects, stakeholders, stages of work, disciplines, deliverables
- add purpose of issue, upload deliverables and create transmittals,
- view dashboard and analytics.

All these transactions are stored on blockchain with timestamp and immutable transaction hashes on a distributed ledger.

(Case study courtesy: Suresh Ram, suresh.ram@infiblocks.com)

CHAPTER 5: CASE STUDY- PRELIMINARY ASSESSMENT IN DESIGN THINKING

Case study (Courtesy: https://www.zeeve.io/)

UK Government is planning to implement Blockchain technology for aiding its food processing industry to offer enhanced trust, traceability and trackability of their goods from raw materials to end product consumption and have invited Blockchain solution provider Zeeve (https://www.zeeve.io/).

What is the information required to be collected as a part of the Design Thinking process?

The preliminary study should aim to understand and formulate the key problems and needs of the customer that helps in testing the formulated hypothesis about the problems and activities that facilitates the solution evolution.

The relevant stake holders are mapped and addressed to gather insights into the current situation. Their problems should be exhaustively listed and insights generated to concretely establish the need and readiness for implementing a Blockchain platform.

The needs of the different stakeholders along with their respective contexts need to be thoroughly understood.

Understanding the context and establishing the benefits of Blockchain in the supply chain Industry:

Blockchain offers the following benefits to the Supply chain industry

1. **Connect siloes:**

A blockchain-validated heads-up display on the health of supply chain will make it easy to know which partners are delivering or are behind. The more information that supply chain stakeholders have about each unit of their associated businesses (and how close to real-time that data is), then the fuller a picture they have about their unknown future.

2. **Increased collaboration:**

Blockchain presents a record of financial tractions in which everyone agrees. Blockchain technology makes it easier to validate the data is real which is much needed for the conduct of transactions between disparate entities from multiple organisations.

3. **Facilitating automation**

Blockchain opens the door to data automation, a key competitive advantage for any business seeking to shake up supply chain thinking and get ahead. Automation can reduce costs and make complicated decisions within the supply chain.

4. **Increased efficiency**

. Blockchain enables lending, financing, and tracking finer details of a business interaction of other transactions by facilitating near instant settlement.

5. **Provenance and Trust**

Blockchain enables a supply chain to track and trace any ingredient or component within the chain from source to production process to the paying customer. It enables verification of the quantity & quality of ingredients they receive, and even gives the ability for the suppliers to conduct recalls if needed.

Assessing if is Blockchain the right choice?

A typical supply chain is characterised by the following

aspects and requirements:

1. There are disparate parties interacting with each other and exchanging value with each other, without a need of a centralized party overseeing every transaction.
2. There is a need for a shared record of contracts, transactions, records in a fully traceable and auditable manner across multiple players in a business ecosystem in a trusted and transparent manner.
3. There are assets having commercial value issued, originated, recorded and transferred across a business network, based on certain process driven activities, that needs to be tracked from issue to end consumption and is the provenance need to be established?
4. There are many parties who exchange private and confidential data as per their contractual engagements and access control levels.
5. Presence of many intermediaries who contribute to delays and cost without adding corresponding value in the guise of mediating trust.

All these points out to clear need to implement Blockchain in a Supply chain scenario. Zeeve created the following preliminary questionnaire to extract the relevant information from the client team to test the readiness of the client and help it to formulate a Blockchain based solution to the client.

The answers to these questions will enable the organisation to assess the impact of implementing the Blockchain platform and to finetune the platform continuously in the maintenance phase,

Business Perspective

1. Identify and list the key problems and challenges that need to be addressed by a platform like Blockchain?

2. List the active/passive participants & all the relevant stakeholder in the supply chain?

3. List the best practices, certification documents and compliances that need to be captured on Blockchain ledger?

4. What are the various access controls to be exercised with respect to the credentials and certifications stored?

5. What all Product & service attributes will be captured in the smart contracts?

6. Who are the other participants such as Insurers, financiers, etc and what are their role is the system.

Process Perspective

This section contains the exhaustive list of internal and external processes that need to be tracked and improvised as a part of the Blockchain platform & solution development. Some of the sample processes are mentioned below:

1. Listing and description of all the processes and activities from the input vendors to the ultimate customers that need to be tracked across the value chain to provide a glimpse of the complete sequence of activities that are undertaken for transformation of the various inputs to the output product/ service.

2 Details of certifications that need to be captured

and presented to their respective seekers for established trust in process/ product quality.

3. The process steps, conditions and business logic that need to be coded into the smart contracts for success conduct of business dealings. The

The logic outlines the access controls, roles and responsibilities of actors and the state changes that happen to all the assets when these logics are triggered and executed.

4. All the various product, process, statutory, compliance, regulatory parameters and SLAs for storage, processing and track & trace paraphernalia like IoT devices, infrastructure etc, should be clearly recorded and documented.

Infrastructure Perspective

All various functional and non-functional requirements and hardware capabilities needed have to be documented.

It is important to understand the type of nodes, their storage and processing requirements, security issues, communication requirements between the different nodes and their respective expected roles with access controls in the Blockchain platform.

Computing infrastructure and devices like servers, computers, laptops, wallets on online or mobile phones. can be become a node connected to a Blockchain system. They communicate with each other through different protocols and update their information on their respective ledgers, based on activities taking place inside the system.

There are different types of nodes like client nodes (that can push transactions and view transaction history), maintainers nodes (that help in validating the transactions or ordering the blocks in a chronological order), oversight nodes that ensure regulatory or platform compliance and administrator nodes that manage the identities and participation authorisation. Depending on the role and data to be maintained or applications to be run, the nodes can be of different capacities.

Nodes can be maintained on different clouds, premises or devices depending on the organisational & participant requirements and are configured according to the needs.

Depending on the need to communicate internally with legacy applications, between themselves and with external entities, there will be several integration requirements. All these need to be noted beforehand before designing the systems.

As we have noted earlier, different types of Blockchain platforms that implement different consensus requirements offer varying capabilities to process the transactions in terms of through put and latency.

All these need to be mapped well in advance to identify the appropriate Blockchain for implementation.

It is possible that a customised platform depending on the information collected and the needs of the customer could be architected that combines the different benchmarked features form the existing platforms.

Some of the key infrastructure elements that need to be understood are as follows:

1. Types of participants who will be hosting a blockchain node along with the approximate number of such nodes. For example, a Blockchain Market place for farmer organisations across the country may have to host lakhs of nodes, while a inter organisations document sharing platform may need to host only a few hundred nodes

with limited transaction throughput requirement.

2. What are the integration touch points, including internal and external parties along with their existing legacy data structures for communication?

3. Where are all the nodes, databases , clients and all the associated infrastructure hosted and what are the requirements for the new nodes that could come into play as the usage goes up?

4. Can we chose from the existing platforms or any new customised platform needs to be created to satisfy the requirements?

5. What are the transaction through put and allowed latency with respective tolerance limits and SLAs? These must be documented and taken care while allowing for the expected growth trends and ability to manage scale in the future.

6. The security, confidentiality and privacy requirements?

This requirement that could warrant varying investments in the security infrastructure, firewalls and establishment of militarized zones needs to be well understood for a fool proof architecture.

The above list is not exhaustive and can vary depending on the situation and the solution architected. The idea of this section is to lead the Blockchain architects to think through all angles, before delving deeper into the design of the system.

CHAPTER 6: IMPLEMENTATION OF BLOCKCHAIN PROJECTS BY GOVERNMENTS

In this chapter, we shall study the use of Blockchain platform in providing e-Governance services and the steps required by Governments to implement such platforms.

Blockchain in E-Governance

Governments offer a number of services to various groups of businesses and citizens and also interact with other Governments. There are a number of departments in the Government which interact directly and also collaboratively with other departments to offer their services.

The paper Consortium blockchain for security and privacy-preserving in e-government systems by Elisa, N., Yang, L., Li, H., Chao, F. & Naik, N. (2019) provides a simple but comprehensive view of a Blockchain based e-Governance system that can be considered for implementation. The choice of the platform could however be decided based on a number of site/situation specific issues like the transaction through put & latency specification, choice of consensus protocol etc.

These services are categorized as follows:

Government to Citizens (G2C) : G2C is the interaction between citizens and government via government web portals

Government to Business (G2B): G2B involves communication between the government and business partners or other corporate organisations to share information such as procurements, company registration and payment for licenses and taxes

Government to its Employees (G2E): G2E can be referred to as intra-government communication concerned with the sharing of the documents among employees of the government.

Government to Government (G2G): G2G is the interactions with other governments as well as the internal communication between government agencies or department by following the established rules governing public services delivery.

While the tremendous proliferation of Information Technology systems has dramatically improved the efficiency of Government systems in providing transparent governance to their constituents, they are also prone to a number of limitations.
Government departments provide services through access points like web and mobile to their citizens. They are prone to various types of cyber security threats and also suffer from the possibility of 'Single Point of Failure' of their backend storage and systems.
History is replete with examples of data breaches that stole the citizen data and the transactional information, with even the occurrence of falsification of asset ownership information, a number of times.

During 2019, data pertaining to about 300 properties in the Karnataka (State in India)'s Kaveri portal was allegedly compromised when some errant officials with technical expertise had misused the portal. This led to the falsification of asset ownership information of a

number ofland records.
Data breaches ofidentity information pertaining to citizens in India and China is well known.

Blockchain platform offers an excellent solution to a transparent and efficient e-Governance , eliminating Single points of failure while derisking the Governments form the loss of precious information.

A consortium based Blockchain platform that connects all the various stake holders and all the Government departments, can facilitate instant validated transactions in a secure and private manner.

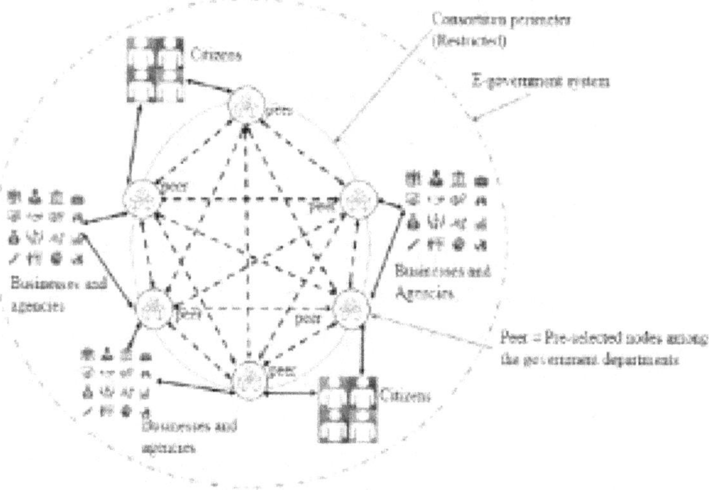

Fig 6.1: Network participants in a Consortium e-Government Blockchain

Individuals and transacting businesses will be offered a Unique Blockchain based ID (UDID- Unique Digital Identity) for accessing all their services from their mobile devices or a desk top device, through an integrated Government portal.
The respective departments validate the credentials of

the citizens and authorise transactions that are committed to the Blockchain ledger.

To protect privacy of the transactions and also to ensure that the Blockchain ledger is not overwhelmed with bulk, immutable data in a short time, data is stored in a ledger data base of the respective department with appropriate replication, while the hashes of the data are stored on a replicated data base across the Blockchain nodes.

A decentralised system comprising of pre-authorised selected nodes approved by the Government can handle the Permissioned consensus mechanism and also ensure that only authorised departments and identified citizens conduct the transactions on the e-Governance Blockchain

The following figure depicts the various layers of a e-Governance Blockchain.

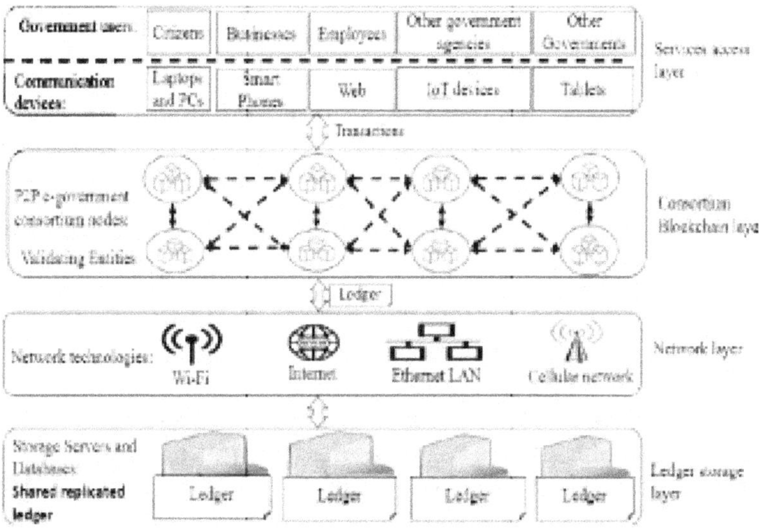

Fig 6.2: Different Layers in a e-Government Consortium

Blockchain

i) Service Access Layer

The purpose of this layer is to enable the delivery of various services to the citizens by the various Government departments.

The user registration process consists of generating a unique PKI based identity after checking the citizen credentials and a unique Public key with a corresponding Private key is generated to identify the user. The user is provided a wallet that can be stored on his/her device through which they can identify themselves and also store their identity & credential related information along with the status of the assets they own as per the current state of the e-Governance Blockchain.

The citizens will be registered and provided a unique common Blockchain based identity to consume and interact with the respective departments through APIs. Citizens can access the integrated e-Governance services portal vide devices like smart phones, PCs, laptops etc. They can connect, interact and store immutable transaction meta data as per pre-configured smart contracts. Sensitive, Private and Bulk data of the respective departments will be stored in off-chain.

Transaction details of all the details are also stored on the e-Governance consortium server to facilitate backup and retrieval in case the user loses the access to the wallet on his/her device for any reason.

ii) **Consortium Blockchain Layer:** The purpose of this layer is to facilitate a collaborative governance of the e-Governance platform by facilitating collective validations of transactions of the transactions by users, through pre-approved consensus algorithms.

All departments of the Government that offer services to different users are pre-authorised by the administrators of the platform and are given a PKI based identity with Public Keys and Private keys that allows them to approve & sign the transactions pushed into the Blockchain.
Thus, only Permissioned users are authorised to take part in the transaction validation & block creation process, while the updated status of the Blockchain is broadcasted to all the consortium participants who are keeping track of the ledger.
The transactions thus approved are immutable recorded on the Blockchain offering verifiability, integrity and non-repudiation, leading to transparency and citizen satisfaction. Users can retrieve and review their transaction status and record any time by using the Blockchain explorer.

iii) **Network Layer:** The Purpose of the Network layer is to connect all the participants, different layers and corresponding storage stations in the Consortium Blockchain electronically by using appropriate technologies like Wi-Fi, Ethernet LAN, cellular network & Wireless Broad Band networks etc. Adequate safeguards like Firewalls, Militarized zones and HSM devices are used to protect the networks across various premises, VMs, devices, VPNs, cloud etc., to ward of any potential security threats and challenges.

iv) Ledger Storage Layer: The purpose of this layer is storing the credential information of the users required to validate them before undertaking transactions and also store a large amount of department specific data that cannot be stored on Blockchain ledger due to privacy and storage considerations.

The integrity of the data is authenticated by comparing the hash of the presented data for a specific record at any point with the hash of the corresponding data stored on the Blockchain, while the actual records are stored in the Ledger storage layer. This layer also allows the compliance of the e-Governance platform with respect to the data privacy laws like GDPR by allowing deletion & revocation when warranted.

This layer is provided the necessary safeguards like replication, high level security and firewalls to ensure isolation from malicious actors.

Blockchain for Smarter & Sustainable Cities

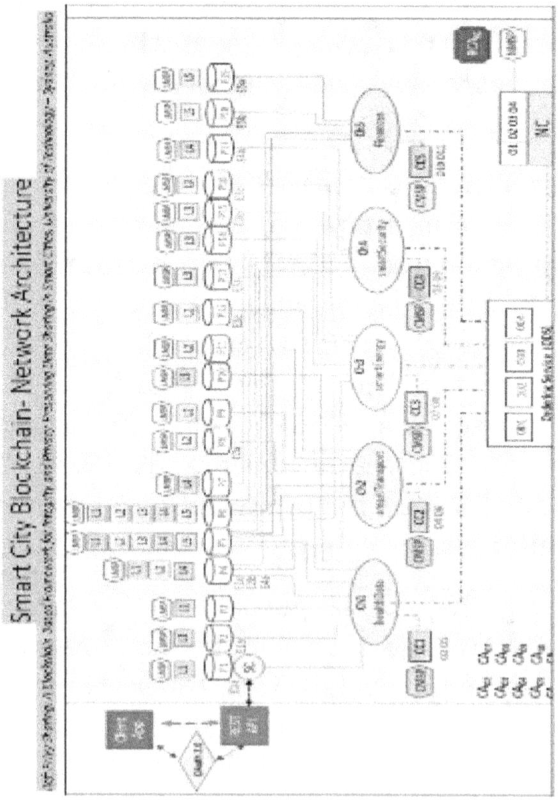

Fig 11.2-2: Smarter cities with Blockchain enabled Privacy & Security

Typical network architecture for a Smart city, connecting various facets of a Smart city can be visualised as in the above figure.

The network members and the operations are depicted as follows:

NC- Network coordinator manages the issuance and control of the Membership of the permissioned parties using NMSP or Network Membership Service Provider.

There are a number of Parties that are permitted to operate on the Smart City Blockchain Platform. The peers P1 TO P 19 are part of respective different organisations that operate through their respective MSPs to manage their identities.

There are different services being provided to the citizens viz.

1. Health record management
2. Smart energy
3. Smart transport
4. Smart security and
5. Financial services

Each of these services are offered through their respective channels (Ch1 to Ch5) created consisting of the corresponding permissioned peers operating in the channels maintaining their respective ledgers (L1 to L5).

Each channel maintains a track of the permissioned members using the respective channel MSPs, operating in the channel through the respective Smart contracts/ Chaincode (CC1 to CC5) being triggered by the respective participants undertaking the transactions that update their respective ledgers.

The network administrators manage the Ordering services that orders all the transaction into timestamped blocks and distributes to the respective channel's leader peers to further propagate to all the peers in the respective channels.

All the members in the network invoke their respective chain code/ smart contract through the client application and upon authentication, trigger the transactions as per their access control through the corresponding APIs.

Thus, the smart city Blockchain network provides an additional layer of security and privacy to the citizens and also leverages the benefits of Blockchain like Tamper resistant ledger and automated operations without any manual intervention to manipulate/ contaminate the recorded data.

STEPS TO IMPLEMENT BLOCKCHAIN PLATFORM DEVELOPMENT BY GOVERNMENTS:

Blockchain being a new paradigm meaning a lot of connotations to different segments of the population, a step-by-step approach has to be considered for going through the planning and implementation phases.

Several risk factors spanning across Technological, Operational and Regulatory domains need to be considered and factored in.

In this chapter we shall understand the various factors and stages of a Blockchain project and also point to the relevant resources which are a must to master for any Blockchain practitioner.

It has happened a few times that, as the projects progressed in real life and after the pilots have been successfully demonstrated, legal issues arose challenging the legality of the Blockchain platform & solution implemented with mistaken notions concerning the Privacy of the data of participants or the eligibility of the implementing parties with respect to the propriety of their involvement in developing solution while taking part in the Governance at the same time. In this case, it must be ensured that there is clear demonstration of the objective nature of governing the platform to ensure no meddling with the encoded logic in the smart contracts.

The various aspects discussed are summarised as follows:

1. Preliminary study and discussions to assess the utility of the Blockchain /Distributed Ledger Technology to the domain specific use cases. Conduct design thinking workshops to understand the problems in the as-is situation, study the processes and improvements required & possible in the desired to-be scenario, conduct gap analysis and plan the solution by leveraging Blockchain.

2. Getting an idea (rough estimate) of the budget that can be allotted for the Project in line with the capacity of the sponsoring organisation or the department/ team behind the project.

3. Creating a DPR (Detailed Project Report) outlining the various aspects of the project in a detailed manner with respect to the planning and design of the solution. Detailed solution architecture and technology stack has to be designed and laid out along with the suggested implementation methodology & the associated risks to be mitigated. Detailed Project Reports (DPRs) are the outputs of planning and design phase of a project. DPR is a very detailed and elaborate plan for a project indicating overall programme, different roles and responsibilities, activities and resources required for the project

4. Creating a Request for Proposal (RFP) for various prospective competent solution providers and system integrators to submit their bids to implement the solution to the expectation of the client as per the terms laid out.

5. Bid management and selection of the right System integrators who can execute the project.

6. Program Management, Capacity building and Change management to ensure that the solution is correctly implemented and delivered with a proper monitoring system in place are the other major steps which have to be executed in a detailed manner. At every stage a thorough testing across all dimensions like regression testing, integration testing, User acceptance testing must

be conducted and bugs taken carefully. DEVOPS methodology that stresses Continuous delivery and continuous integration enables a smooth project execution that minimises risk and overall costs.

For interesting reports on implementation of Blockchain projects in Government, please download papers by WEF, PwC, E&Y etc., from the link https://drive.google.com/drive/folders/1efmhzh5pmvxr0unMz6gKlzQhii2vlBI5?usp=sharing or write to bct4nip@gmail.com.

Case study:
Implementing Blockchain for e-Governance

Understanding the utility of Blockchain for citizens:
Problem: The problems that citizens face on a day-to-day basis are well depicted in the following figure.

Fig 6.3: Fake documents, identities, products plaguing the citizens leading to a lot of leakage of lives and money

As we have seen Blockchain offers solution to these problems and improves quality of governance by making Processes and their transactors:

- Transparent

- Instantly Verifiable
- Accountable
- Tamper proof
- Near real time
- Eliminates fakes
- Minimise Paperwork

Some of the important government services that can be automated & securely delivered through a Blockchain are:

- Land Records: Creating a new system to manage authentic land record transfer and ownership
- Securing Government issued certificates and documents
- Pharmaceutical drugs supply chain through blockchain enabled trust
- Blockchain solution for educational certificates
- Immunization Supply Chain
- A blockchain based model for subsidies and benefit transfers
- Tracking and Provence of Organic Farming
- Securing energy trading through Blockchain
- Secure payments and transactions in immutable records and many more.

This calls for Government founded Blockchain that is

- Enterprise grade
- Offers G2G, G2C, B2B services
- as a Blockchain Backbone
- with Smart Contract Capability

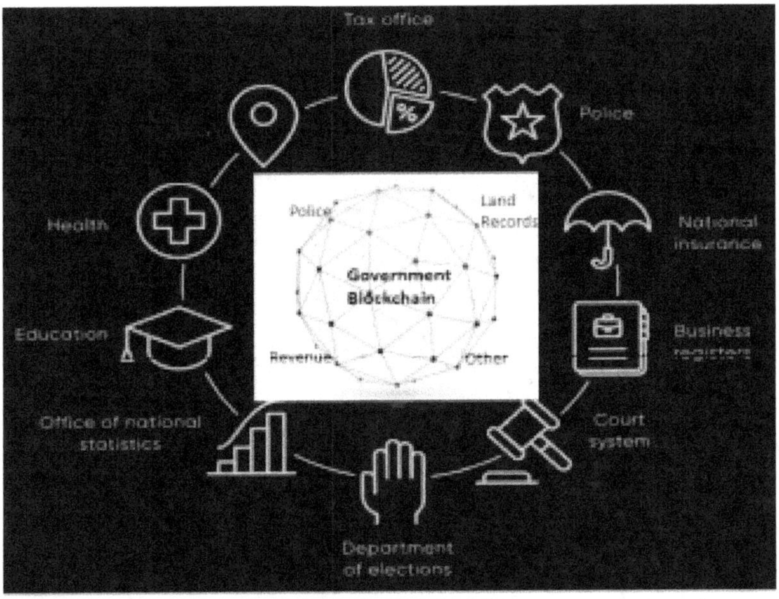

Fig 6.4: e-Government Blockchain Backbone connecting departments with citizens and businesses

The reference model for offering e-Governance services over a Blockchain by Consensys is depicted below:

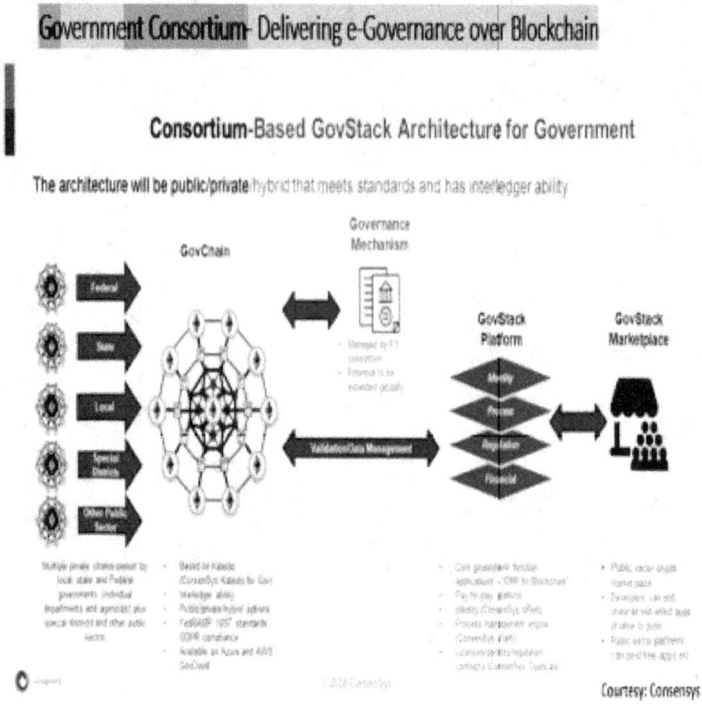

Fig 6.5: Blockchain based e-Governance reference model as depicted by global leader Consensys

Some of the key components of the Blockchain are:

- Web App Layer
- RPC API validation
- Block Explorer
- Node Stats Monitor
- Wallets
- Re-usable DAPPs
- RPC Nodes for connecting with Blockchain
- Pre-Approved Trusted Authority Miner nodes

The technical architecture of the Blockchain platform can be depicted in the following diagram.

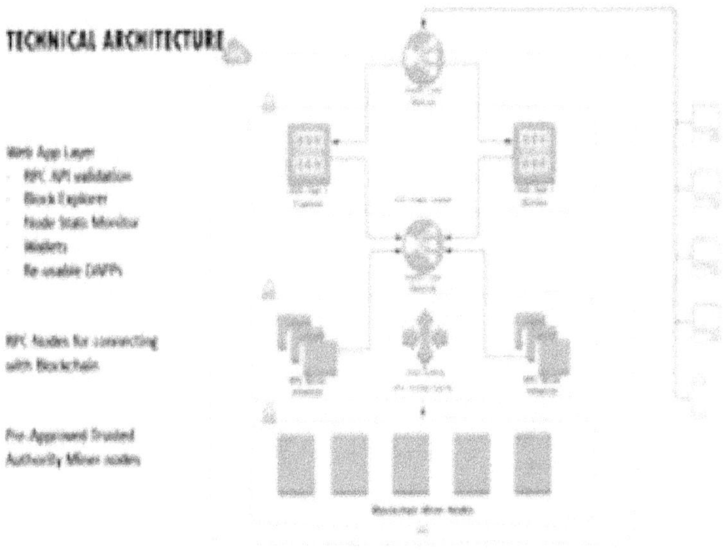

Fig 6.6: Technical architecture of the Blockchain platform

Implementation of Blockchain platform by Governments to deliver services to citizens involves integration of nodes of various departments with the overall platform, various layers that provide admin, authentication, security services, application layer, external and on-chain storage layers etc.

Adhichain a Public permissioned platform anchored at Chennai, India, has created a functional reference model for Government Blockchain that can be depicted as in the following diagram.

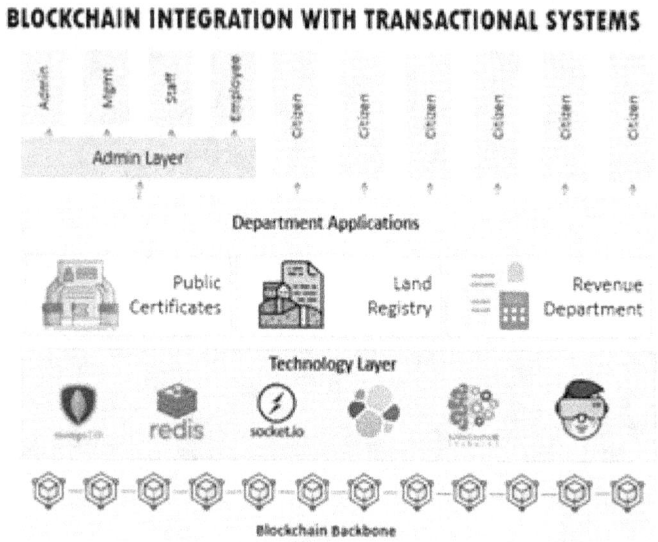

Fig 6.7: Integrated & simplistic view of a Government Blockchain platform (Courtesy Adhi Chain, India

Since different departments have different legacy systems with their own specific data formats, it is imperative that, Blockchain platform offers a facility for the respective department by the use of an Adapter that converts the legacy data format to a format (example JSON, Xml etc.) that can interact with the Blockchain.
This can be done in 2 ways:

a) Blockchain platforms issues a standardised data format to the various partners pushing/ consuming the data through APIs.
This imposes a need for the respective departments/ organisations to build their own adapters and communicate with the Blockchain Nodes.

ii) Blockchain platform offers a customised adapter to each and every partner that enables seamless communication.

The following diagram depicts the schematic approach of the communication through an adapter service for data compatibility and interoperability with the legacy systems and the same can be extended to the interactions across different platforms as well.

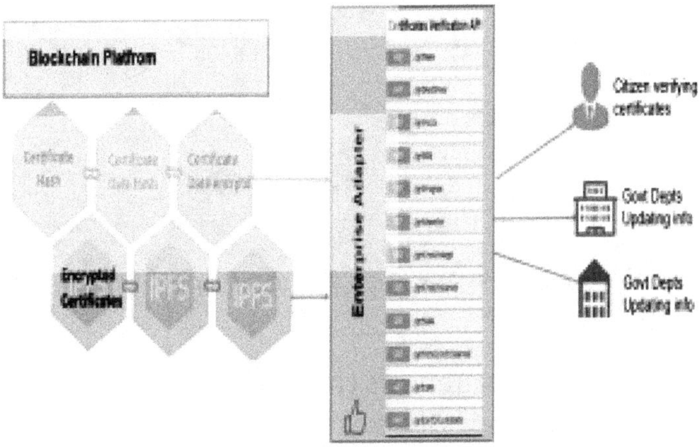

Fig: 6.8: Adapters facilitate seamless inter-operability between backend systems

Depending on the privacy requirements, the following are the options available to store the data in the form of a 'meta data' or its hash encrypted format.

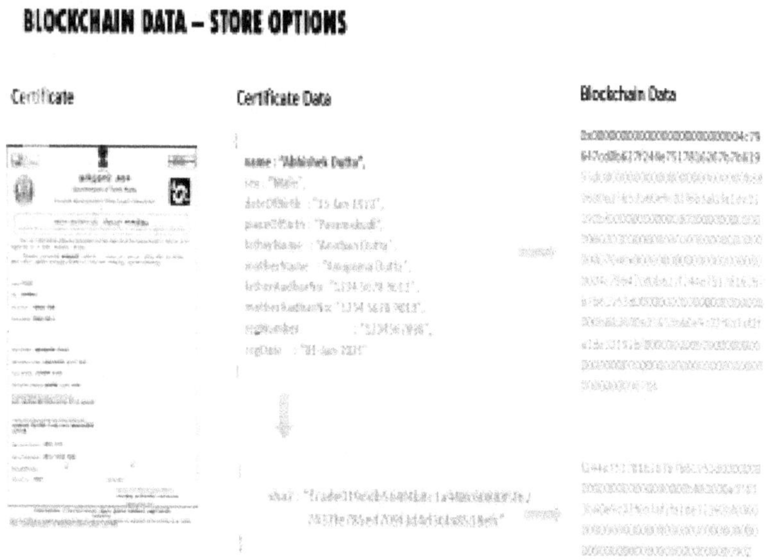

Fig 6.9: Data store options to meet Privacy requirements

Some of the documents that can be digitised and stored on the Blockchain platform operated by the Government can be as follows:

- Aadhaar card, a biometric, digital and physical identity system.
- Indian passport
- Overseas Passport
- Electoral Photo Identity Card (EPIC) issued by the Election Commission of India
- Overseas Citizenship of India document
- Person of Country Origin Card
- Permanent account number (PAN) card (income tax)
- Driving licence issued by the states
- Ration card issued by the Government of India
- Identity Certificate for non-citizens or stateless people

- Proof of Marriage document issued by the Registrar
- Legal Name Change Certificate
- Birth certificate issued by the Registry of Births and Deaths (RBD) or from a Municipality within the provisions of the RBD Act
- Policy Bond issued by Public Life Insurance Corporations/Companies
- Community certificates
- Freedom Fighter Identity Cards
- Arms Licenses
- Property Documents such as Pattas, Registered Deeds etc.
- Gas Connection Bill
- Bank/ Farmer/ Post Office Passbooks
- Photo Bank ATM Card
- Photo Credit Card
- Pensioner Photo Card
- Certificate of Identity having photo issued by Gazetted Officer or Tehsildar on letterhead
- Unique Disability ID (UDID) Card / Disability medical certificate issued by the respective State / UT
- Marriage Certificate

To transact with the Blockchain , the users are provided wallets to store their assets and credentials. A typical Blockchain platform comes with the following minimum components for offering Trust as a service to the various applications anchored on it.

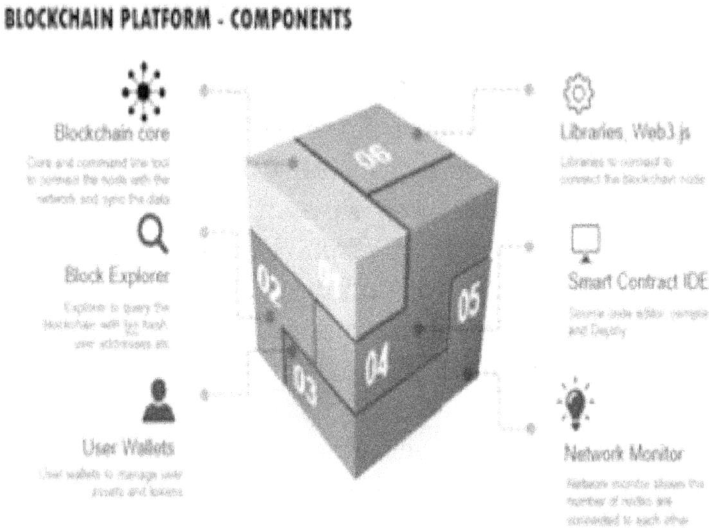

Fig 6.10: Blockchain Platform components for a holistic solution delivery

In the coming chapter, we shall examine how some of the leading global countries are encouraging the adoption of Blockchain in their countries through the creation of a friendly regulatory and technology patronising environment that lets the disruptive technologies take wings in offering the beneficial impact to the citizens.

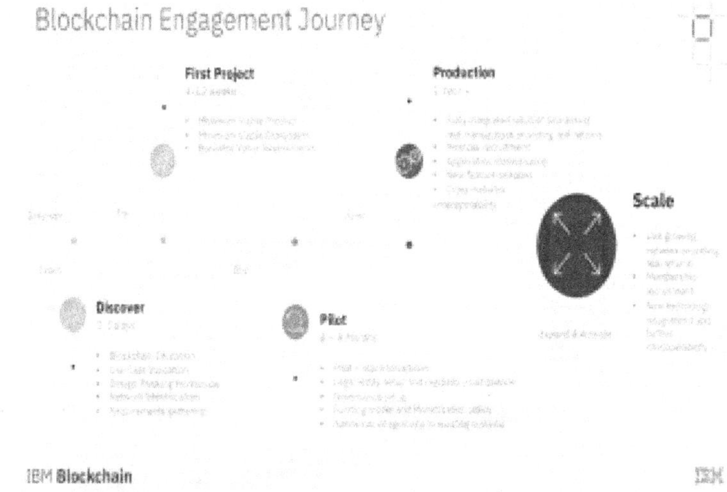

Fig 6.11: IBM's guidance for Blockchain engagement timelines

Creating a Detailed Project Report for a Blockchain Project

It is said that 90% of the project fail due to improper planning. Hence before we embark on any project, a detailed architecture and a comprehensive road map needs to be created with attention to minute details. As discussed earlier, Detailed Project Reports (DPRs) are the outputs of planning and design phase of a project. DPR is a very detailed and elaborate plan for a project indicating overall programme, different roles and responsibilities, activities and resources required for the project.

An excellent resource to understand the various phases of Blockchain implementation is provided by American Council for Technology-Industry Advisory Council at https://blockchain-working-group.github.io/blockchain-playbook/phases/4/

Fig 6.12 : Blockchain implementation Playbook (ACT IAC)

The following are the key components of a DPR for a Blockchain Project.

1. Objective of the Project:

It is very important to have a clear understanding of and communication about the reason behind the project. 5W &1H, the approach that describes the 'Why What, For Whom, Where & When should be described in clear detail with shared understanding between all the stake holders.

2. Understand and analyse the Stakeholders:

A thorough analysis of the various stakeholders operating in the ecosystem along with their interactions with the Blockchain platform & motivations for change must be documented. Analysis and insights from this stage have a bearing on the solution design and feasibility.

3.Project Implementation Strategy.

Once the DPR is approved, Government and PSU organisations undertake a standardised methodology for executing large scale project. The phases of the project along with their expected timelines should be outlined to arrive at a proper effort estimate.

The phases that have to be planned are as follows:

i) Create a Request for proposal and invite vendors to quote

ii) Conduct Pre-bid meetings to clarify and correct errors.

iii) Check the technical competence through demonstrable Proof of Concepts.

iv) Select the right vendor partner/consortium for awarding the contract & onboard the same.

v) Execute the project by overseeing the implementation of the vendor partner from design stage to final testing & roll out.

vi) Roll out the Pilot in a limited scope and ensure its adherence to the requirements.

vii) Scale out the project and complete the execution at full scale successfully. This is the major phase that generally takes 50% of the total time.

At every stage the prerequisites for the stage and activities during the stage need to be mapped out in detail.

4.Functional Solution

The functional solution is the heart of the entire project. It lays out exactly what, the system is expected to deliver.

It involves detailing the data models corresponding to the actors, the assets and their ownership, the processes that are undertaken for the state changes that need to be represented in the Smart contract applications.

All the various modules corresponding to the various applications along with the requirement of their user interaction/ user interfaces & the corresponding functionalities need to be understood and outlined clearly.

5. Identity Management

Identity management will involve the ways in which the participants are identified in the Blockchain platform.

The access, authentication and authorisation particulars of the various participants and the corresponding processed through the transactions are undertaken by them are outlined in detail.

In general, the identity of the participants is established through a three-factor approach that taken into account what they are (Unique National Identity like Aadhar), Biometric details like Iris, fingerprint), what that possess (card with details embedded in a chip) and what they know (one-time Pin).

Blockchain offers a full proof identity establishment with the help of PKI based authentication, multifactor authentication and digital signature-based message authentications to fix accountability, integrity of data and non-repudiation. This has crucial implications for the utility of Blockchain platforms.

6. **Change Management**

Blockchain being one of the latest paradigms that offers a paradigm shift in the way we approach business transactions; it is bound to trigger a lot of scepticism and resistance to change. To overcome this, there is a need to educate and bring on board all key stakeholders & the users of the system.

Lucid lessons and training material coupled with benefits explained to all the participants will go a long way in effecting the change management smoothly.

Hence capability building is a key component and must involve all concerned parties in the ecosystem and those involved in the project implementation. This is a pre-requisite for project success and is a key component of

DPR.

7. Governance Structure

Blockchain is adopted for its role in creating trusted and transparent transactions. The transactions between multiple parties in the ecosystem are recorded permanently. Blockchain is governed by a Network governing committee composed of cross functional leaders & other responsible representatives, to collectively take a call on the participant additions and deletions as well as changes to the contract structures.

Many times, consortiums fail due to the partisan approach of the governing team or wrong decisions and misgivings. The following teams form the various elements of governance that need to be carefully identified and managed.

- Network governance team that involves all the leaders and provides the regulatory & audit oversight as required to ensure compliance,
- Platform implementation sponsoring team, that helps in getting the necessary budget support and financial clearances required for execution
- Project management team that ensures effective delivery and monitoring across the various phases of execution and
- Functional team comprising teams taking care of application development & monitoring, technology, security, partner management.

8. Operations Management

Operations management involves taking care of all the issues during the functioning of the application and the platform operation. While care is taken to ensure that there are minimum errors and failures possible through different types of testing before releasing, any issues that are springing up anytime should be logged and monitored for satisfactory closure as per SLAs.

Appropriate software, monitoring, reporting and logging tools and Helpdesk with 24 by 7 capability to record, address the issues through a systematic escalation mechanism must be planned for.

To ensure security, it is important to consider Security by Design and implement proper firewalls, VPNs and HSM modules etc., to adhere to Confidentiality, Integrity and Availability all times.

9. Technical Design:

This involves:

1. High level design showcasing the interactions between various layers of the system viz., Blockchain layer & Data layer, Business logic layer and the Presentation layer.
2. Access control for participants and security aspects
3. Details of On-chain & off-chain applications and data elements,
4. Smart contracts for each process flow and the detailed functionality of each of them.
5. Different nodes and their quantity & design elements like size, location, role etc., for various levels of implementation

10. Transaction Estimates

The type of Blockchain application and the use case decides the throughput and maximum latency expectation. The Blockchain platform and the hardware impose the capability of the system to handle the same. Hence it is extremely important to have a clear understanding of the volume and the size of the transactions expected to be handled by the system in a 1-year time frame that can be deduced to the level where it can be used to compare with the corresponding handling capacity of the platform. For example, Permissionless platforms like Ethereum and Bitcoin are tremendously limited by their capacity in handling the enterprise requirements in most cases. Hence Permissioned applications are the way to go for G2C or G2B applications.

11. Risk Management

Large scale IT projects that involve huge investments are susceptible to different types of risks that can jeopardise the returns on investment. Hence a proper assessment of the different types of risks and the corresponding mitigating mechanisms must be factored in, without which the DPR is assumed to be complete.

Technological and Operational risks, external risks and regulatory risks have to be factored in and taken care, while planning for the Blockchain Projects.

12. Final Project Estimates.

The cost estimate for the project factors in all the elements considered above. A typical output of a Detailed Project Report offers the estimate based on all the functional and non-functional requirements and the respective volume estimates and assumes the following heads:

- Effort towards the development of the various application elements including smart contracts and their integration with the front-end various modules as explained earlier .
- Cost of hosting nodes and the various hardware elements including the application and web servers and all other associated paraphernalia.
- Cost of HSM/ VPN/ Firewall/ Security/ Racks/ Data centre Infrastructure
- Maintenance cost and operational expenses including IoT devices, gateways, QR codes, Active/ Passive RFID

tags etc.

· Detailed estimate of Training and Capability building required to onboard all stakeholders till final implementation.

Most of the times, Government projects require definitive costing for budgeting instead of on a pay per unit or pay per use model, that is normally preferred for private sector players.

Though a few the above costs could be fixed in nature depending on the volume estimates, some of the costs like hardware or platform licenses and that of packaged software and their maintenance could be costed on variable basis and has to be appropriately budgeted.

The next steps involve creation of RFP (Request for Proposal) through the various stages leading to the final implementation.

World Economic Forum has come out with a suggested model RFP template that is well described in the documents available at the link:

https://drive.google.com/file/d/1p_vwXfbFOdABYmrGOIlcGXrv7AcNM_KI/view?usp=sharing

(mail at bct4nip@gmail.com)

CHAPTER 7: DESIGNING A BLOCKCHAIN PROJECT- CASE STUDY

Puducherry Government wants to implement Blockchain based solution for transparently managing the distribution of its Civil supplies to beneficiaries who are qualified citizens. They have requested Civil chain company to design a solution for the project. Here is briefly how, they go about it.

Civil supplies play crucial role in upliftment of the society. Civil Supplies Department is entrusted with the responsibility of ensuring that ration and other social benefits as directed by the Government reaches the intended customers.

Increasing government schemes demand for transparency in the civil supply chains. Civil supply chains involve dozens of personnel and hundreds of interactions with high probabilities for human error and mismanagement.

Blockchain technology promises to improve traceability and transparency within the civil value chains. Blockchain technology has the potential to make civil supply chains more secure, transparent and efficient. It promises end to end supply chain visibility and allows to trace the origin of a produce (provenance) and track a product/produce during its journey in a supply chain.

In this chapter, we propose blockchain based supply chain tracking and tracing solution which can help in improving efficiency and effectiveness of the current civil supply value chain.

1. Understanding the process:

Currently Civil Supply value chain involves the following process:

1. Food Producer or Merchant transports the commodity/product to the Warehouse via Transporter
2. Warehouse transports the commodity/product the retail ration shop
3. Beneficiary buys the commodity/product at subsidized price

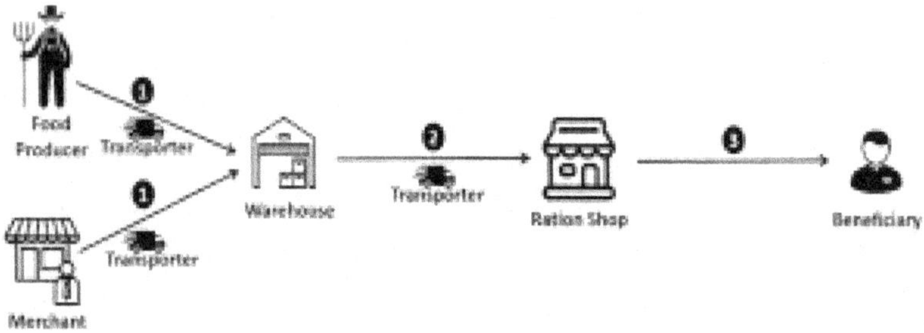

Fig 7.1: Understanding the Civil supplies Supply Chain

Defining the Problems and understanding the pain points in the value chain:

Civil supply value chain's efficiency and effectiveness decreases due to the following issues:

i) Lack of coordination across multiple, disbursed and often disconnected supply chain actors like suppliers, transporters, warehouses, ration agents etc.

ii) Lack of consistent data and digital capabilities making sharing of information across the Supply chain difficult.

iii) Onerous and costly data reconciliation processes

iv) Lack of product/commodity traceability

v) Manipulation of information stored in the records. For e.g., subsidy information etc.

vi) Injection of counterfeit or substandard commodity/product in the supply chain.

Analyzing the proposed solution requirements and describing the same:

Solution Objectives:

- Digitize all the transactions taking place in the entire Civil Supply Value Chain.
- Track commodity/product from point of purchase to the point of sale at ration shops.
- Tamper proof and single source of truth for all the transactions & product's/ commodity's attributes throughout the Civil supply chain.
- Timestamp each transaction in the supply chain.
- Near Real time audit of the system and the processes.

Components of the Solution architecture are as follows:

The solution development considers the following:

i) Data model : It is important to clearly identify the different data elements that are a part of the entire lifecycle tracking of the assets and transactions.

ii) The identities of the actors, things being tracked, their roles must be tracked with the following elements:

a) ID of the element,

b) Description of the element

c) Information capsule about the element - that undergoes additions, deletions and state changes due to the transactions being conducted through the triggering of the smart contracts at various points.

d) Types of transactions and the corresponding resultant states of the objects participating in the transaction along with the transaction IDs are key data element to be tracked in the Blockchain.

The solution architecture incorporates the following views:

i) Case View: Case view tracks the different sequences of activities, their corresponding actors & their respective roles.

ii) Logical view: Logical vie takes a look at the various stages, packages and steps in the process of development. This gives a clarity of the overall requirements of the system being developed.

iii) Process view: Process view offers a detailed look at the different processes that need to be configured in the form of smart contracts and their description.

iv) Deployment view: Deployment view involves the depiction of the various hardware and middleware that enable us to launch the application securely. The various nodes, security and networking elements and their interaction is depicted in this view.

v) Implementation View: Implementation view provides the overview of the different options for implementing the technology and the advantages and disadvantages thereof. In this book are focusing on the elements concerning the designing of the solution. For more details on the implementation aspects refer to the Blockchain implementation Playbook by ACT-IAC available at https://blockchain-working-group.github.io/blockchain-playbook/phases/4/ .

Proposed Solution description:

- Proposed solution is a Blockchain based digital supply chain tracking & tracing solution.
- Blockchain network & shared ledger between different participants in the civil supply value chain

Depicting the Solution Workflow:

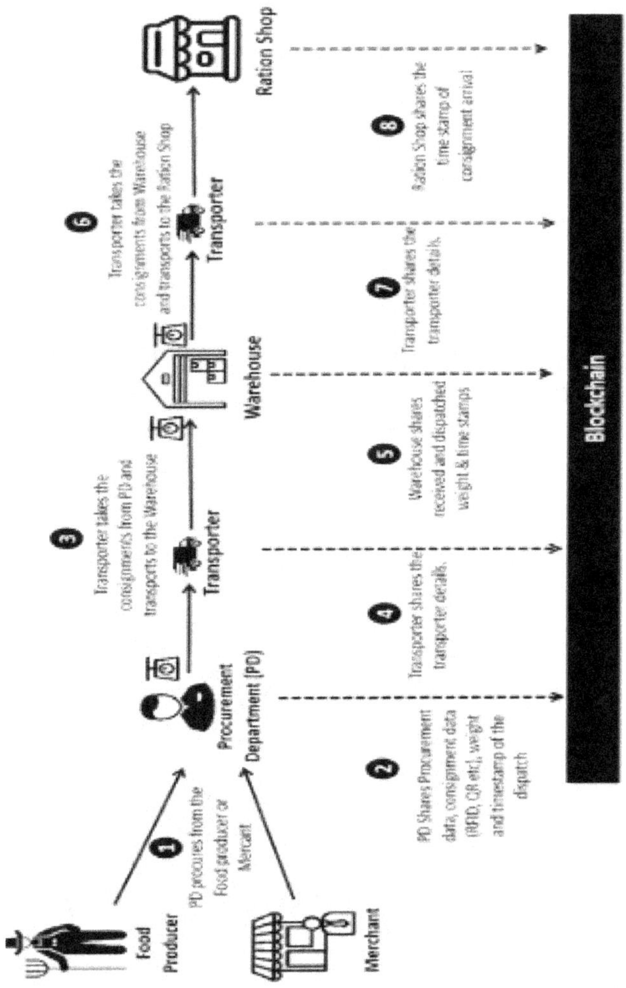

Fig 7.2: Outlining the solution workflow process

The above process flow can be understood in detail from the following table, describing the different steps.

Process description of Civil Supplies Value chain

Sr. No	Process	Process Description
1	Harvesting/ Manufacturing	• Farmer harvests the produce and segregates it into the gunny bags • Merchant packages the goods into gunny bags
2	Procurement	• Procurement Department (PD) procures the commodities/products from farmer or from the merchant. PD registers following details for each of each gunny bag in the web/mobile app: ▪ Supplier (Farmer/Merchant) details ▪ Quantity stored in the gunny bag ▪ Quality details of the product/commodity • Once the gunny bags are registered, QR code is generated automatically. PD prints the QR code and sticks to the gunny bags. • PD collates multiple registered gunny bags and creates a consignment. Each consignment box is secured with thermocouple and polymeric sensor and a passive RFID tag • PD checks weight of consignment box before shipping and feeds in mobile app • Consignment also gets the QR code which is invisibly linked to the QR codes of the gunny bags in the consignment. • Smart contract is initiated when the consignment is shipped
3	Transportation to warehouse	• Transporter picks up the consignments from the PD and deliver to the warehouse • Passive RFID tags enter a time stamp at the start of the journey and a time stamp at the end of the journey at the warehouse • Any violation of the expected time taken or tampering of RFID/ QR code of the consignment will be dealt with as a violation of a smart contract on the blockchain.
4	Warehouse storage	• Warehouse scans the RFID tag and QR code on the consignment via mobile/web app. Time stamp of the scanned event is captured in the blockchain automatically. • Received consignments' weight is measured at the weighing bridge and the same is recorded in the blockchain via mobile/web app • Any deviations in the measured weight (exceeding the accepted deviation range) from that fed by the PD triggers alerts and violation of smart contract
5	Transportation to Ration shops	• Consignments dispatched by the Warehouse are weighed and the same is recorded in the blockchain via mobile/web app • Any deviations in the measured weight (exceeding the accepted deviation range) from that fed by the warehouse at the receiving time triggers alerts and violation of smart contract • Passive RFID tags enters a time stamp at the start of the journey and a time stamp at the end of the journey at the ration shops • Any violation of the expected time taken or tampering of RFID/ QR code of the consignment will be dealt with as a violation of a smart contract on the blockchain.
6	Consignment received by the Ration shop	• Ration shop owner scans the RFID tag and QR code on the consignment via mobile/web app. Time stamp of the scanned event is captured in the blockchain • Consignment's weight is checked and recorded in the blockchain. • Smart contract verifies entered weight against its original weight recorded previously in the blockchain. If the weight of the consignment is not equal to the weight recorded earlier in the blockchain, alert is triggered and results in smart contract violation.

Table 7.1: Describing the Process flow in Civil Supplies Value chain

For implementing the above process flow on a Blockchain platform, the following layers are required.

Sr No	Component's Name	Description
1	Front end layer	The Web/mobile interface will be used for the purposes of the front end layer; however the same would have to incorporate the following (detailed would be determined as per the integration requirement gathering during implementation) : • Separate web/mobile interface for Procurement Department • Separate web/mobile interface for Warehouse • Separate web interface for Transporters • Separate web interface for Ration shops
2	Blockchain layer	Blockchain network will be created with following properties: • Network set up for Nodes : ○ Admin node to be hosted by the Civil Supplies Department ○ Node for warehouse department ○ Representational node for transporters to be hosted by the Civil Supplies Department ○ Representational node for ration shops to be hosted by the Civil Supplies Department • Wallets for all the participants in the network. All interactions between participants will happen through their wallets. • Permissioned Ledger. Only participants approved by the admin will be permitted on the network. • Smart Contracts

Table 7.2: Key Solution components

Front end layer: This is required for participants to interact with the Blockchain system and other application components as per their access control terms.

After an analysis of various Blockchain platforms with respect to the characteristics of the scenario depicted, it has been felt that a Public Permissioned implementation with Hyperledger Fabric is the best fit for the given use case.

The Web/mobile interface will be used for the purposes of the front-end layer; however, the same would have to incorporate the following (detailed would be determined as per the integration requirement gathering during implementation):

Sr. No.	Component	Description
1	Finance	Gathers financial data (price, taxes etc) related to transaction at each stage of the Civil supply valuechain.
2	Web and Mobile API	APIs to integrate web and mobile applications to the system of the proposed solution
3	Log Management	Logs of all the requests and responses to them received from all the front end interfaces
4	Any other module	Further components can be added as per requirements that will be gathered post award

Table 7.3: Application Service layer modules

- Separate web/mobile interface for Procurement Department
- Separate web/mobile interface for Warehouse
- Separate web interface for Transporters
- Separate web interface for Ration shops

The Blockchain layer consists of the following components:

Sr. No.	Component	Description
1	Distributed Ledgers	Ledgers or databases distributed across the peer to peer network to store the consignment's change of ownership data and other attributes at each stage
2	P2P Messaging	Peer to Peer communication system and protocols
3	Wallet	Application to store the private and public keys of the node. All communication of the node happens via the wallet.
4	Smart Contracts/Chaincodes	Smart contracts to ◦ Track weight of consignment throughout the civil supply value chain and trigger alerts in case of deviations exceeding the accepted range ◦ Track consignment's ownership changes throughout the civil supply value chain ◦ Trigger alerts when time taken in transportation exceeds the accepted range ◦ Trigger alert if warehouse or ration shop scans the RFID tags &/or QR codes not registered previously by the PD.
5	Ordering Service	Gathers and orders the transactions in block and broadcasts the blocks to the peer nodes to include the same in their ledgers
6	Certificate Authorities	Issues PKI based certificates to the network member organizations and users
7	Channel	Private blockchain overlay that allows data isolation and privacy of the data. Each channel has their own ledger.

Table 7.4: Blockchain layer components

Blockchain network will be created with following properties:

- Network set up for Nodes:
  - Admin node to be hosted by the Civil Supplies Department
  - Node for warehouse department.
  - Representational node for transporters to be hosted by the Civil Supplies Department.
  - Representational node for ration shops to be hosted by the Civil Sup-

plies Department

- Wallets for all the participants in the network. All interactions between participants will happen through their wallets.
- Permissioned Ledger. Only participants approved by the admin will be permitted on the network.
- Smart Contracts

Implementation of the Blockchain based Supply chain Solution offers the following benefits to the Government and the various users of the system.

S No	Value	Description
1	Tamper Resistance	Entire trail of custody transfer of the consignment from point of procurement to ration shops is captured in Blockchain which makes the system incorruptible
2	Tamper evident system	Blockchain based system maintains a natural log of all the transactions which will be provided as a traceability log at the admin/Civil Supplies Department's interface
3	Helps in reducing black market sales	Blockchain based system efficiently tracks every consignment procured throughout its civil supply value chain. Any illegal consignment if entered in the system in the intermediary stage can be automatically notified to the Civil Supplies Dept. by the system
4	Transparency	Since all the transactions taking place in the civil supplies value chain are captured in the blockchain and stored in tamper proof manner transparency is ensured by the proposed solution
5	Real time auditability	Blockchain stores only authentic and authorized transactions and hence reconciliation of transactions is almost instantaneous.
6	Shorter lead times	Blockchain provides the platform for real time data sharing leading to shorter lead times, reduced redundancy, and fewer delays
7	Streamlined operations	Digitization of the workflows and automation through the smart contracts results in streamlined operations.
8	Prevent product/commodity leakage/diversion	Consignment level tracking on blockchain's tamper proof platform prevents any sort of leakage or diversion
9	Less scope of fraud	Consignment level tracking in tamper proof manner and resultant transparency in the system leads to reduced scope of fraud in the civil supply chain

Table 7.5: Benefits of implementing Blockchain system for Civil supply value chain

Components of the Technology stack for implementing the Application architecture for proposed solution includes the following:

1. **Firewall**: The proposed system will be maintained by firewall to filter out the invalid requests.
2. **Load Balancer**: Load balancer redirects the incoming requests based on the load on the corresponding web servers
3. **Presentation Layer** contains the web and mobile interfaces
4. **Application Server Layer** of the proposed solution contains the following components:

Elements of the architecture	Tech stack description
Front end	Web (React.js) and Mobile (Angular)
Back end Application	Node.js
Blockchain	Hyperledger Fabric
Language used for Blockchain script	Go/Java
Database - Presentation Layer - Application Layer - Blockchain Layer	 Postgres SQL Postgres SQL Proven DB/IPFS/Mongo DB
Message Queuing system	RabbitMQ
Load Balancer / Web server reserve proxy	Nginx
Security protection	Firewall & IDS system for protecting the network traffic & access controls

Table 7.6: Technology stack components

To implement the above components, we need to configure the following elements of the solution architecture and shown in figure 7.3 viz depicting the deployment view.

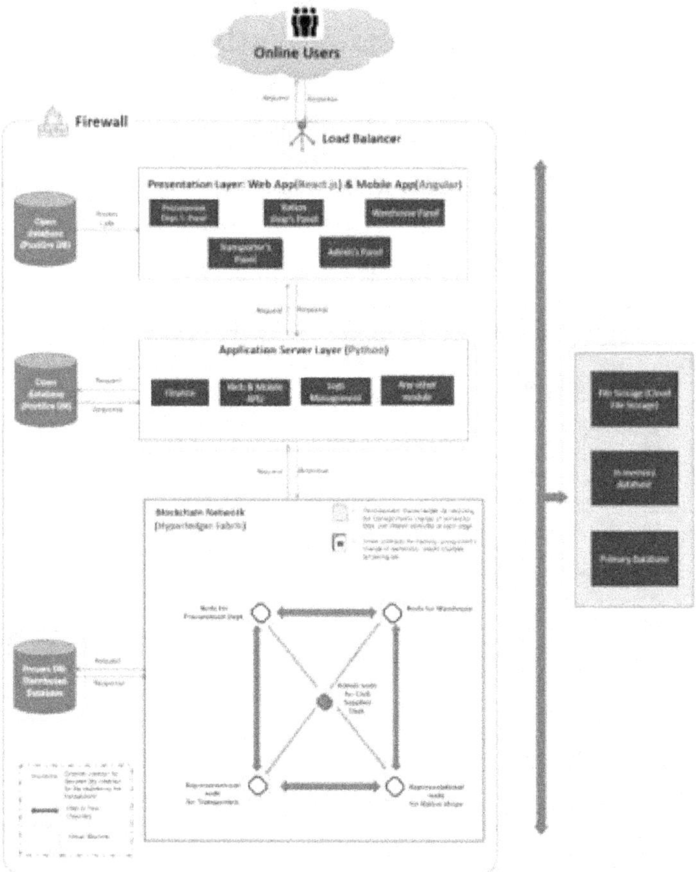

Fig 7.3: Deployment view of the Solution architecture

For the given use case, the details of the specifications of the technology components can be summarised as follows:

Sr. No.	VM	Hardware Type	Cores	RAM (GB)	Storage		
					Size	Type	RPM
1	VM 1	Blockchain Node 1	2	32	500 GB	RAID 5	Greater than or equal to 10K
2	VM 2	Blockchain Node 2	2	32	500 GB	RAID 5	Greater than or equal to 10K
3	VM 3	Blockchain Node 3	2	32	500 GB	RAID 5	Greater than or equal to 10K
4	VM 4	Blockchain Node 4	2	32	200 GB	RAID 5	Greater than or equal to 10K
5	VM 5	Application Server	2	32	1 TB	RAID 5	Greater than or equal to 10K
6	VM 6	Centralized DB	8	64	500 GB	RAID 5	Greater than or equal to 10K
7	VM 7	Blockchain DB	8	64	1 TB	RAID 5	Greater than or equal to 10K
8	VM 8	Load Balancer	8	64	500 GB	RAID 5	Greater than or equal to 10K
9	VM 9	ESB	2	32	500 GB	RAID 5	Greater than or equal to 10K
Total			36	384	5.2 TB		

Table 7.7: Hardware sizing and specifications

Security Aspects of the Proposed Solution

Architecture of the proposed solution supports the following features to enhance security performance:

1. **Permissioned blockchain**: Identities joining the network must be approved by the network administrator. It is always advisable to create a policy for admitting new members in the network. Also, network members have to approve for any change in network configuration or to deploy smart contract.
2. **Privacy & Confidentiality**: Proposed solution make use of Hyperledger Fabric which ensures data privacy and confidentiality with following features:
    a. Channels are sub networks within the larger blockchain network for scoping and data isolation. Ledger

& smart contracts maintained within a channel can only be accessed by the members of that channel.

b. Channel private data allows for finer security within the channel by allowing data access to selected few members within the channel. In such cases, the blocks on the ledger only contain hashes of such data, while the private data is stored off the ledger in a private state database. The hashes on the public ledger serve as verifiable proof of the data.
c. Data can be hashed or encrypted before calling smart contract.
d. Data access to some participants can be restricted by defining access control in the smart contract logic
e. Data stored in the ledgers of peers can be encrypted via file system encryption on the peer
f. All communication

between different nodes is encrypted via Transport Layer Security (TLS)

3. **Identity Management**: The system makes use of industry standards for digital identities i.e., X.509 certificates. At its core Hyperledger Fabric is public key infrastructure (PKI) system. Certificate Authority is responsible for registering new users to the network and issue them X.509 certificates. Membership Service Provider (MSP) manages the access management for different identities in the Fabric application.
4. **Transaction integrity**: Propose solution uses cryptographic techniques to prevent transaction tampering.
5. **Data security**: Data is arranged in blocks and blocks are linked with previous blocks using hash pointers. Thus, data stored on blockchain ledgers are cryptographically secured by design.
6. **Smart contract security:** In Fabric smart contracts or Chaincode are installed on peers and explicitly initiated. When initiated, each Chaincode runs in a separate and isolated environment called Docker container. In Fabric, an operator can configure a policy to disable all outgoing or incoming network traffic on the Chaincode Docker containers, except white-listed nodes.

Security Risk Assessment of the Proposed solution

Following table summarizes common security threats and how a Blockchain based solution mitigates the same.

Sr. No.	Threat	Threat Description	Mitigation
1	Spoofing	Unauthorized users gains access to the system either pretending to be authorized user or stealing user's private key	Certificate Authority generates X.509 certificates for all the members. Network protocols ensure the certificate revocation list distribution among all the participants to ensure that revoked members can no longer access the system.
2	Tampering	Modify the information entered in the database	The system uses cryptographic techniques (like SHA 256, ECDSA) to make tampering infeasible.
3	Repudiation	An entity can deny the action performed by it later on	The system tracks who did what using digital signatures.
4	In-transit Data Leakage	Information can be intercepted by third party when in-transit.	The system uses TLS v1.2 for in-transit encryption of data.
5	Replay attacks	Repeat/Replay transactions to corrupt the ledger	Read/write sets are used to validate the transaction before adding to the ledger. Thus, a replay of transactions will fail due to an invalid read set.
6	Denial of Service	Malicious users makes network resources unavailable to the legitimate users	The system prevents DOS attacks through strong identity management and access control policies.
7	Erroneous smart contract	Malicious or erroneous smart contracts can corrupt the network, risking theft or exposure of private data	The system executes the smart contracts in docker containers for sand-boxing. Also, the network admin has option to limit the access and run docker containers with appropriate restrictions.

Table 7.8: Security threats as addressed by a Blockchain based system

It is now time to take a look at the Implementation view. The proposed solution is planned to be implemented in 14 weeks as depicted in the following Gantt Chart. These needs to finetuned further once detailed scoping and solution discussions are undertaken and the final deployment plan emerges.

The implementation schedule also allows the implementation partner to estimate the effort and quote for the final budget requirement to implement the project.

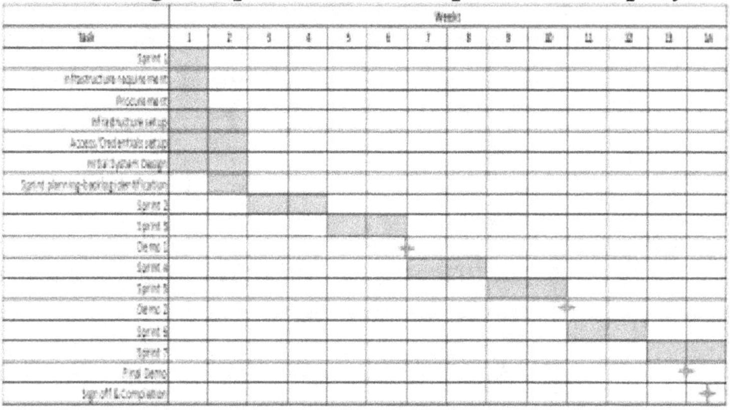

Fig 7.4: Gantt chart depicting the tentative implementation timelines

As we can observe from the above chart, best approach is to use the Agile methodology involving a series of short sprints.

Implementation of an end-to-end blockchain solution involves engineering both the infrastructure solution and the application solution that runs on top of the infrastructure solution.

The infrastructure solution involves heavy investments and it cannot easily be changed. The architecture should be modular, reusable, and extendible options whenever possible. Given the rapid transformation in the blockchain technology space, what works today may become a significant burden or even obsolete in 3-5 years. In that sense, rapid prototyping with constant iterations is the preferred way of implementing blockchain solutions.

During the Implementation Phase, you should use a systems-engineering approach to further refine the detailed design and architecture of the blockchain solution. This may involve evaluating and making or refining decisions regarding at least some of the following:

- Choice of the development platform, technology stack, tools ecosystem.
- Commercial of the shelf versus in-house.
- Open Source versus proprietary solution.
- Cloud, on-premises, or a hybrid deployment architecture.
- As-a-Service solution.
- Network architecture and network registries.
- Business process flows.
- Consensus algorithms.
- Design of blocks, distributed ledger databases, data.
- Design of transactions.
- Design of smart contracts.
- User interface/user experience design.
- Leverage machine learning, artificial intelligence.
- Interoperability with legacy and third-party systems/data.
- Privacy.
- Rules and policy engine.

- Cross-blockchain architecture and interoperability.
- Non-functional requirements.

Agile and DevOps methodologies are highly recommended for the project management approach. Included in that is the management of the scope for your blockchain solution implementation.

Agile development provides an iterative roadmap where implementation is done in small increments. Achieving incremental gains satisfies stakeholders while enabling you to strategically scale so that you can optimally address pain points, while tackling one priority area at a time, to ultimately accomplish transformational objectives and advance mission goals.

(Source Blockchain implementation Play book- ACT-IAC)

Risks and Mitigation:

As discussed earlier, Blockchain being a new paradigm that is dramatically altering the way we look at inter-enterprise co-operation and collaboration led digitisation, leveraging network effect and affecting the entire ecosystem, one needs to be caution and plan for different risks involving Operation, technological, regulatory and external risks. A sample approach to estimating risks and planning for the risk mitigation is described in the following table.

S. No.	Risk Description	Mitigation
1	Requirements are not well defined	Requirements gathering workshop before finalizing the requirements
2	Inadequate client team involvement	Business and Technical teams should meet and engage regularly
3	Changes in requirements	Clear change management process should be agreed before the start
4	Infrastructure requirements are delayed	Exact infrastructure requirements can be finalized in requirements gathering workshop. However, we can work on our local servers till the provisioning happens
5	Blockchain technology is new	Though blockchain technology is immature, our experienced experts have track record of successfully implementing blockchain solutions globally.
6	Difficulty in onboarding the participants	Initially the onboarding may be enforced by regulation, however later on participants can be motivated to join the network by giving incentives
7	Difficulty for participants to adapt to the new system	Training and workshops should be conducted for all the participants to educate them about the system. Also Training manuals and video lectures should be made available to all.

Table 7.9: Risks and mitigations- A sample approach in a Blockchain project

With the above approach, the Blockchain solution development company can provide the necessary roadmap to the Puducherry Government to undertake a Blockchain implementation for implementing a transparent Supply chain and prevent leakages, while maximizing the benefits to the needy citizens.

In this chapter, we have taken a look at the different stages of Solution architecture that will enable us to architect the solution, take a look at its different views. Though this is a bit simplistic approach, the different situations call for a corresponding variation in the micro level components that go into estimating the final effort and the budget required for the Blockchain based solution being designed.

CHAPTER 8: BLOCKCHAIN AND GOVERNMENTS- EXAMPLES AND CASE STUDIES

Citizen Identity Management

Identities and digital signatures for Access, Authentication and Authorization are the critical components of a Blockchain paradigm that provide the critical 'Security,' 'Privacy' and 'Confidentiality' to the participants in the network.

Problems identified : Multiple records, Duplication of efforts and processes, Siloed systems and potential for identity fraud and that of stolen credential copies.

Solution offered by Blockchain:
Issue and verify once on Blockchain, link multiple identities to a unique Blockchain identity-operated through a single user interface or a digital wallet, eliminate the need for multiple verifications across establishments thus saving a lot of time, effort and documentations which maximizes the trustworthiness of the identity information.
The Identity Management of citizens is a very important facet of the individual's rights. However, the multiplicity of interactions and the potential unauthorized use of personal information in an indiscriminate manner for commercial purposes open a Pandora's box of ethical issues along with personal security concerns. Blockchain offers a unique Digital Identity Management system that offers the safety and security of their personal data and allows the members to provide permissions to users of the identity information. The concept of self-sovereign identity and decentralized key management

system offered by platforms like Hyperledger Fabric, Hyperledger Indy, Uport or Aurigraph etc., enables the organizations to register members uniquely over a Public Permissioned network.

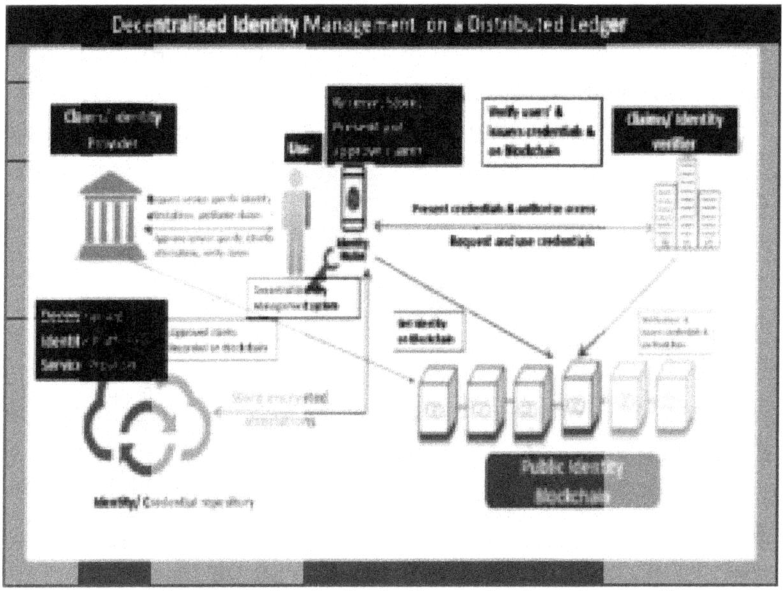

Fig 8.1: Blockchain based Identity and Credential Management System

The Government and its various departments will be able to access data over a National DLT platform while being able to track and trace data and transactions from heterogeneous platforms in one infrastructure.

The National DLT backbone would offer a seamless platform for verified Citizen, Business and Government interactions that would be shared on a public ledger while maintaining requisite privacy.

6 Businesses can use the same platform for other functions such as license applications, employee background checks, compliance reporting, credit check and loan applications. Government notifications may also be delivered on the same system.

Government Services

The Government may offer a suite of digital services to Businesses and citizens. These could include processing applications and petitions directly handling and delivery. The Government may choose to deliver notifications and alerts directly to businesses and citizens with a digital auditable trail, delivery confirmation and read receipt that may be linked to Smart Contract for follow-up action.

The Government services could also include tracking of criminal activities and records from all departments and security agencies as a centralized database would be impossible to maintain.

Governments may also conduct elections and surveys at a fraction of cost and infrastructure used today while ensuring the integrity of the data collected and its immutability. The results would be reported immediately after closing hours with the count being taken in real-time.

Use Cases involve collaboration among users, businesses and Government for delivery and consumption of services. The Roadmap starts with decentralized identification infrastructure, authenticating citizens and business and aggregating their respective documents from the issuers in the users' Digilocker account. Users can issue and consume documents and services securely from the same Digilocker as a service. Examples include:

1. Citizen Identity Management across decentralized and heterogeneous sources
2. Land records, Building plan approvals, tax assessments and payments and the consequent bank reconciliation
3. Permits and Licenses issued in compliance with regulatory provisions for various purposes to citizens.

4. KYC processing for citizens and business entities
5. Employee background verifications
6. Employee payments with salary, income tax, provident fund and professional tax reconciliation
7. GST reconciliation across a value chain for input tax credit
8. DBT Track-and Trace under Central and State sponsored schemes to beneficiary

Zero-Knowledge Proofs allow the members to selectively disclose their identity without revealing confidential information. For example, the ZKP system allows the member to prove that he/she is above 18 years without the help of a Pan card or reveal his/her Bank balance is above Rs 10000/- without revealing the actual account details that could be confidential information.

Estonia, considered one of the most digitally advanced countries, has put in place a comprehensive digital identity verification platform for its nation's citizens, where citizens identified through their access card with identities registered on a Blockchain can access any of the Government and most private services and provide conditional access to their credentials that identify them without disclosing too many private details. The citizens' identity is used by the Government and private sector to provide safe, secure and private access to their personal health records and also participate in different voting activities. An insightful coverage of Estonia's Blockchain implementation is provided at the following link:

https://www.ctga.ox.ac.uk/sites/default/files/ctga/documents/media/wp7_martinovickellosluganovic.pdf

Voting

Problem: Tedious manual paper and printing intensive processes requiring humongous funds and fake/unaccounted identities pose enormous challenges for countries and enterprises undertaking elections for governing bodies and on-board resolutions.

Solution offered by Blockchain

By uniquely identifying voters in a fool proof manner and recording their votes through their digital signatures through a verifiable and non-refutable system, Blockchain eliminates fake votes, wrong votes and extensive paperwork eliminating wasteful processes to reduce costs enormously.

Registries and Certificates

Problem: Fake certificates and high cost and time required for issuance and verification plague documentation of events from birth to will execution for asset acquisition and credential accumulation.

Solution offered by Blockchain

Educational Municipal, Police and other credential certificates can be issued and shared securely eliminating fakes and offering benefits for instant audit and reconciliation while establishing clear title.

Benefits and Subsidy Distribution

Problem: Fake claims, excessive middle layers leading to leakages and adding non-value costs drain valuable resources of Government and trusts.

Solution offered by Blockchain

Clear identification of beneficiaries, allotment and monitoring of benefit utilization for every unit issued with minimal intermediary intervention in near real-time allows for high productivity of welfare spends.

Supply Chain

Problem:
Procurement: Subjectivity and opaque procurement processes create leakages and mistrust.
Financial Documentation: Letter of Credit, Suppliers credit and other financial transactions offer a lot of scope for manipulation and mistrust.
Provenance: Fake goods and wrong claims for premiumness hamper a variety of goods ranging from Pharma, food, imported, exported and specialized products
Retail: Warranty claims, Loyalty rewards cross multiple vendors are difficult to track and often lead to disputes
Transport conditions: Un-monitored cold storage transported goods like pharmaceuticals, food, milk and dairy products lead to the consumption of spurious/expired products.
Solution offered by Blockchain
Transparent and Trusted processes offered by immutable, shared ledger of records between verified identities.
Digital signatures for non-repudiation and shared ledger for near-real-time communication drastically reduces costs and scope for frauds.
Smart contracts triggered to capture the events like a change of ownership and transfer of assets immutably on a shared ledger, help identify the origin of the products along with certifications of the originality of standard adherence, especially valuable in Automotive spares.
Blockchain facilitates seamless tracking of warranty claims and allotted rewards until redemption for increased effectiveness and benefit of consumers.
By recording the temperature of cold-stored items across the supply chain and tracking them on a Blockchain ledger, the consignment details of spoiled items

can be quickly traced. This will minimize the propensity of wilful manipulation.

Health Care

Problem: Fake drugs, Compliance in Clinical record management, health record tracking and settlement of insurance claims are often causes for fraud and manipulation.

Solution offered by Blockchain

Blockchain can offer multiple benefits for solving the various challenges of health care domains like seamless management of EHRs with utmost privacy and security features, transparent compliance tracking in case of clinical records and insurance settlement and Origin-to-chemist tracking of Pharma goods, etc.

Smart City

Problem: Unauthorized access by cybercriminals to leverage net connectivity of the IOT devices for DDOS attacks and illegal actions like crypto-jacking, data leaks, etc. The command and control of autonomous vehicles and drones need to be secured against cybercriminals.

Solution offered by Blockchain

Blockchain offers a protective shield for IOT Gateways, autonomous vehicles, drones and robots and prevents unauthorized access by criminals and manipulators. This enables secured automation. Blockchain facilitated accurate assessment of renewable energy claims and peer-to-peer energy trading among Prosumers.

Cybersecurity

Problems: Single points of failure of centralized management offer valuable targets for cybercriminals. Increasingly digitization and billions of internet connections managed by centralized systems run the risk of derailment and ransom attacks. WannaCry, one such virus infected 230,000 computers in over 150 countries, using 20 different languages took $300 US Dollars per computer to decrypt and release the data.

Solution offered by Blockchain

By sharing distributing data across multiple ledgers, authenticating identities, encrypting transaction information, Blockchain offers a de-risking mechanism for data-intensive applications and blunts designs of Ransomware criminals who fraudulently sneak into corporate systems, encrypt the data and demand ransom to decrypt the same.

The utility of Blockchain in eliminating fakes through trusted document management and ensuring source to destination ownership tracking can be succinctly summarized in the following lifecycle activities that could be authentically stored on a Blockchain:

Cradle to Grave/Womb to Tomb – All certificates in one's life from birth certificates, vaccination records, Health/ Property and Academic, Non-academic and Identity records, Will recording and execution, etc., need impeccable tracking that Blockchain provides.

Vivad to Viswas – Any agreements and compliance issues can be easily reconciled.

Farm to Fork/Catch to Consumption – Safe and compassionate handling of animals and amphibians meant for consumption can be tracked through the supply chain.

Procure to Pay – Complete transparency in the Procurement process by recording activities in every stage. Procurement is the biggest source of subjective behaviour that can be made transparent.

Pay to Cash – Manpower and work outsourcing organizations can minimize Pay-Bill cycle leakages by instant settlements and eliminating the need for reconciliation.
Admission to Retirement– Academic and non-academic certificates and transcripts can be stored and shared privately without any fear of fake certificates and time loss.

Segregation of Duties: In issues of Project management or execution of shared responsibilities in organizations, IT projects and new product development, there is a need for responsible and automated tracking of discharge of one's duties. Digital signatures and non-repudiation help in achieving instant confirmations and recognition of good and productive behaviour.

Start-up valuation and compliance tracking: Most of the small companies suffer from the inability to capture value contributions and tracking from the promoters and investors. Blockchain enables perfect, real-time valuation, promoter shares' tracking and support in compliance management for the Start-up founders from the idea stage itself.

Sanction to Settlement: Many activities in Government and enterprise domains need approvals and endorsement. Blockchain can track the documentation and attestations from approval to settlement in an impeccable manner. House designs, Police approvals for public meetings, large project budgets are some of the many such activities that can benefit from the Blockchain approach.
The following solution depicts a typical document management solution by leveraging Blockchain technology to eliminate fake certificates and facilitate trusted shar-

ing of information guaranteed by Blockchain while protecting from malware attacks and any form of unauthorized tampering.

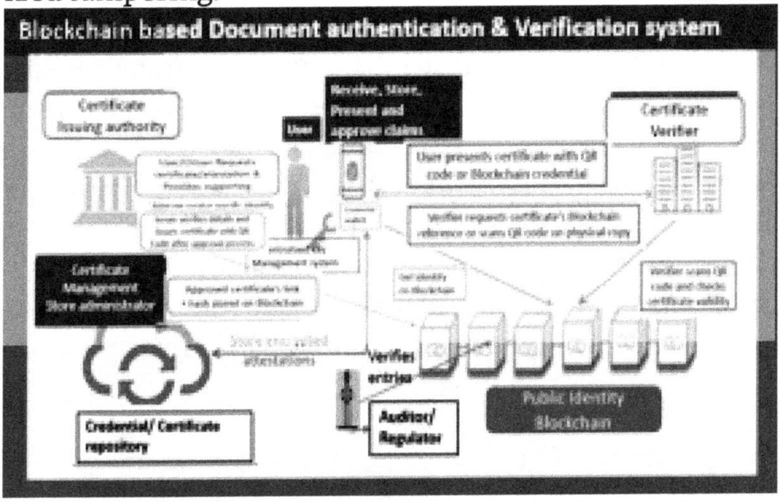

Fig: 8.2 Blockchain-based Instant Document management authenticity verification system.

Loyalty, Games and Sweepstakes and many more applications that depend on Trust are lifelong relationships between hitherto unknown parties cutting across domains, will find Blockchain an interesting platform to adopt and provide value to the peers on either side.

Blockchain can also help in a variety of Smart City applications to save lives and improve quality of life. The following case study showcases the use of Distributed Ledger Technology to seamlessly connect various actors in a smart city ecosystem to improve emergency healthcare response.

1Collaborative Smart City Emergency Response for Smart cities:

Smart cities in India have implemented various 'smart' elements across several dimensions to automate various aspects of the lifecycle of a citizen's interactions with the Government. To facilitate smooth coordination between the citizens and the smart elements present in the city, ICCC (Integrated Command and Control Centre) has been set up by all the smart cities.

However, the communication among all the smart elements is still lacking coordination especially with respect to a timely and coordinated data sharing.

Faced with one of the highest numbers of traffic deaths across all the megacities of India at 157 per hundred thousand of population, Bhopal has sought to leverage Distributed Ledger Technologies to integrate various elements of its Emergency Response actors and their activities.

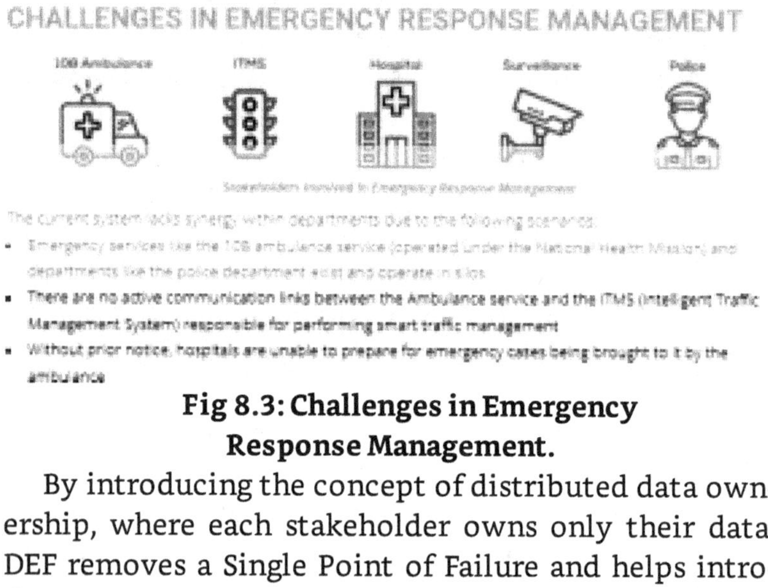

Fig 8.3: Challenges in Emergency Response Management.

By introducing the concept of distributed data ownership, where each stakeholder owns only their data, DEF removes a Single Point of Failure and helps introduce trust among all stakeholders. Stakeholders are able to transparently share information with an immutable audit trail of each transfer The ICCC is able to streamline the city's Emergency Response service with other departments such as the traffic management system, hospitals, surveillance systems and the police.

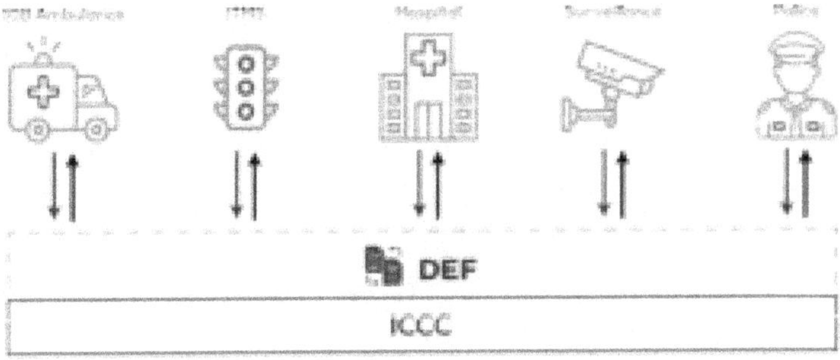

Fig 8.4 Data exchange framework of ICCC to connect all the players in Emergency Response team(Source: Somish Solutions Ltd.)

By implementing a shared ledger by leveraging Distributed Ledger Technology, the Smart City of Bhopal's ICCC was able to create a rapid response to any emergency by the ambulance service to any accident case that is being reported by the citizens. The process flow is described below:

1. The citizen reports an incident via the 108 Helpline.
2. As the ambulance is dispatched the case details are shared with the relevant hospital, ensuring the staff has enough time to prepare for the emergency case.
3. The ICCC (Integrated Command and Control Centre of the Smart City) o is informed of the incident location and designated hospital, which activates the ITMS to create a traffic-free route leveraging the surveillance, public announcement and traffic management systems.

This establishes coordination among stakeholders, increased inter-department synergy and significantly faster transit time by triggering a green corridor for the ambulance transit.

The Smart City of Bhopal, in association with the Institute of Development Studies and National Institute of Urban Studies, successfully concluded the pilot in collaboration with Somish Solutions Ltd and is planning to expand the pilot for wider implementation.

Case study: Courtesy, Somish Solutions Ltd, New Delhi

typical network architecture for a Smart city, connecting various facets of a Smart city can be visualised as in the following figure.

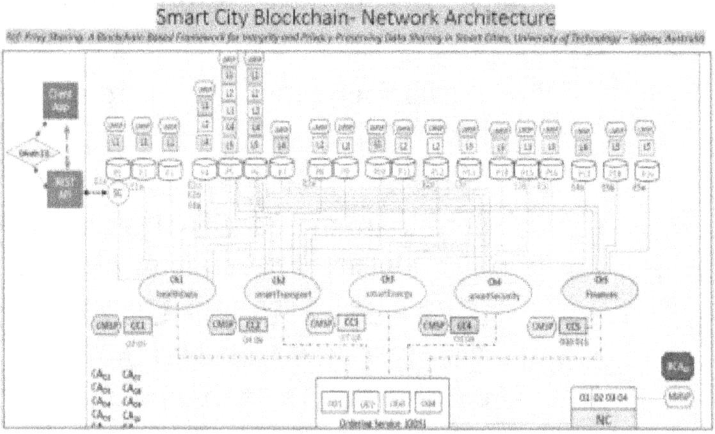

Fig 8.4.1: Smart city Blockchain Network architecture over Hyperledger Fabric (Courtesy- University of Technology, Sydney-Australia)

<u>Secured Access and Management of Autonomous Vehicles, Drones and Robots Using Blockchain</u>

Autonomous driving vehicles are expected to come onto roads in large numbers and are an amazing extension of IOT technology combined with artificial intelligence and machine learning applications. However, they are extremely vulnerable to hacking by cyber criminals. Blockchain offers the best possible security to the autonomous vehicles to ensure that, they are not manipulated and their owners are not held to ransom.

In December 2017, an exciting disruptive technology company, XAIN and the global leader in automobiles, Porsche announced a partnership to take Blockchain technology to the management of cars.

XAIN and Porsche successfully tested a proof of concept in which an Ethereum client is fused to the car's systems and is connected to the Blockchain network comprising of IPFS and BAAS nodes in the

azure marketplace. The car is tracked and managed through smart contracts and owner wallet present in the smartphone of its owner. The car's systems are tracked and all the parameters recorded in the vehicle

wallet that keeps track of various aspects about the car's performance and activities etc.

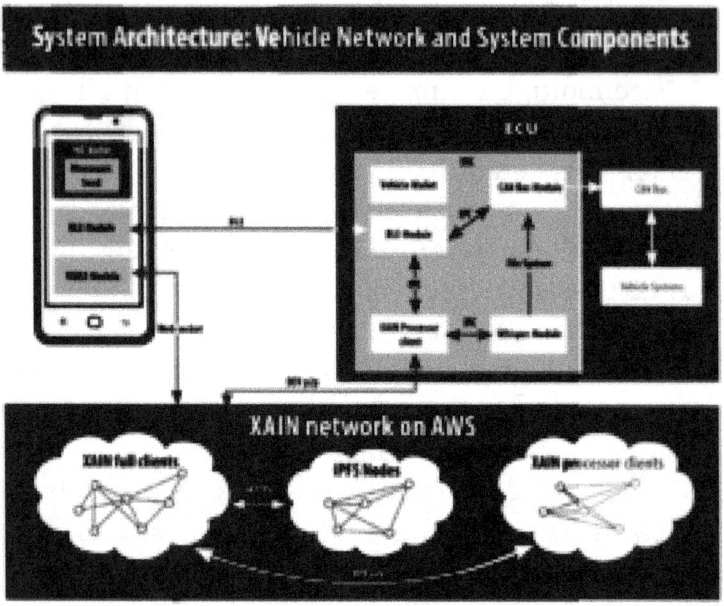

Porsche - XAIN Vehicle Network System Architecture

Fig 8.5 System architecture of Blockchain powered car management implemented by Porsche & XAINFigure courtesy: Porsche Digital Lab (https://medium.com/@ porsche_tech)

Source:https://medium.com/next-level-german-engineering/theporschexain-vehicle-Blockchain-network-a-technical-overviewe1f48c40e73d

The system will allow the authorized owners to access and communicate with their cars using the smartphone connected to the network and do the following from anywhere in the world through internet or through Blockchain powered direct offline connection in a secure manner:

●● Lock, unlock doors and luggage compartments from distance securely,

●● Communicate with other cars in the network and exchange information,
●● Record and manage all critical information on a decentralized trust less system and
●● Prevent hacking by cyber criminals.

Another interesting use case is that of managing the autonomous vehicles like drones for the welfare of citizens and protection of these vehicles for unauthorized hacking to use them for illegal & criminal activities. One such illustration is given in the following section.

CONTROLLING DRONES THROUGH BLOCKCHAIN FOR SECURITY & AUDITING

According to a study by Transport Systems Corporation UK, a research conducted by them along with Sheffield University offered a breakthrough solution for controlling Unmanned Aerial Vehicles by using Blockchain. Ability to control Drones, track and record their movements immutably and issue instructions only through secure authentication and access protocols can assist the security authorities in controlling illegal drone activities and ensure that the flight information can be audited & all safety standards can be adhered to.

This can also lead to substantial improvement in usage of Drones for a variety of applications including ecommerce deliveries, media and movies etc.

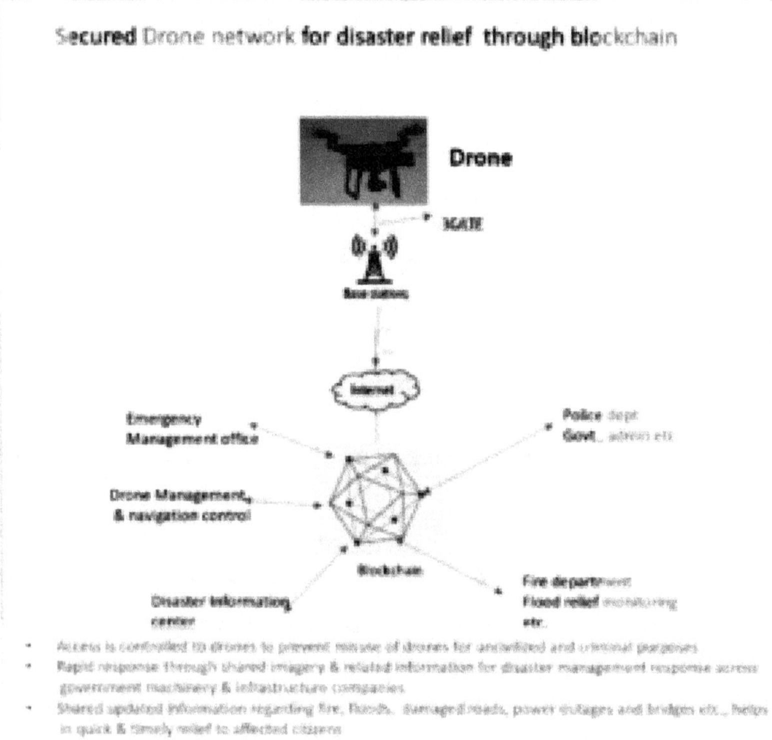

Fig 8.6 Secured Drone Management using Blockchain

The Blockchain based backend system allows access to, from and between robots in a safe and secure manner so that no malware attackers and unauthorized cyber-criminals have access to the agents of automation to cause havoc to the mankind.

This also reminds of Technological Singularity, a hypothetical moment in time when any physically conceivable level of technological advancement is attained instantaneously. At this point which many experts predict to happen within the next 20 years, the self-directed computers will develop super intelligence with their intelligence increasing exponentially rather than incrementally. This, in case if it really happens, is expected to transform the life on

earth and can also enable them to find solution to many human problems including disease and mortality.
The only way in which this level of intelligence that is already growing exponentially to be secured and controlled is through the risk management and protective powers, the Blockchain technology offers.
The internet of Robots marketplace secured through Blockchain allows for a safe and secured access to ensure that proper verifications
and multi-level protection is provided to the Robots to ensure that they are used only for helpful and positive activities that benefit the mankind. The same can be extended to all autonomous objects for a
breakthrough management in a secured manner, as shown in the figure on 'Decentralised Management of Autonomous objects through Blockchain.'

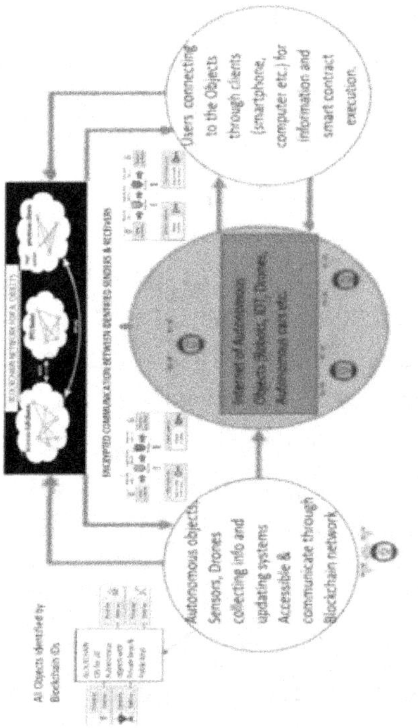

DECENTRALISED MANAGEMENT OF AUTONOMOUS OBJECTS MANAGED THROUGH BLOCKCHAIN

Fig: 8.7: Blockchain marketplace to Securely access Autonomous objects, Robots and Drones

Central Bank Digital Currency Projects

Another important Blockchain influenced application that can accelerate Smart city projects by facilitating digital value transactions between connected things and humans, while helping in unlocking the value of the data generated is the Central Bank Digital Currency Project.
Currently, the US Dollar is seen as the globally interoperable currency accepted by most nations. In the recent past, several countries are experimenting with the concept of leveraging the internet for speedy transfer of value considering the impending
proliferation of IOT & Industrial IOT-led Home automation, Industrial automation and Smart City projects across the world. There has been a strong need felt for a digital equivalent of the national currencies giving rise to the concept of Central bank digital currency (CBDC), also called digital fiat currency (a currency established as money by Government regulation or law). Central Bank Digital Currency is different from virtual currency and cryptocurrency, which are not issued by the state and lack the legal tender status declared by the Government.
Various countries are already experimenting with the concept of CBDC and it is considered a transitory step to the ultimate eventuality of a fully digitized currency with the added security measure offered by
a Blockchain approach.
According to the BIS, today some 70% of central banks are looking at CBDC, with most of them considering Blockchain as the underlying technology.
Some of the global Distributed Ledger Technology-based

CBDC projects disclosed in the public domain are given in the following table published by Bank of Thailand in their project report on the state of
CBDC project being experimented by BOT in conjunction with R3 Corda, Indian IT major Wipro and several trans-national banks.

Phase	Paper Published	Project Focus	DLT Platform Used
Bank of Canada		Project Jasper	
Phase 1	Mar. 2016	1. Create a wholesale interbank RTGS proof-of-concept on DLT Ethereum platform 2. Evaluate PFMIs against tokenised interbank payments	Ethereum
Phase 2	Dec. 2016	1. Rebuild original proof-of-concept on Corda 2. Build additional functionalities such as LSM	Corda
Phase 3	Oct. 2018	1. Integrate a liquidity savings mechanism for netting transactions 2. [illegible] DvP solution for security settlement	Corda
Monetary Authority of Singapore		Project Ubin	
Phase 1	Aug. 2016	1. Build a proof-of-concept for domestic RTGS on a private Ethereum network 2. Identify the non-technical implications of moving this into a production environment 3. Integrate DLT with existing RTGS in a test environment to automate tokenisation and detokenisation	Ethereum
Phase 2	Jul. 2017	1. Expand on the original proof-of-concept by incorporating LSMs 2. Understand how RTGS privacy can be ensured on DLT 3. Compare alternative DLT platforms	Quorum, Corda, Hyperledger Fabric
Phase 3	Nov. 2018	1. Explore different combinations of DLT for DvP between cash and Singapore government bonds 2. Test and evaluate solutions designed by Anquan Capital, Deloitte, and Nasdaq	Ethereum, Hyperledger Fabric, Chain, Quorum, Anquan
Central Bank of Brazil			
Phase 1	Aug. 2016	1. Identify use cases and build a working prototype for the central bank using DLT 2. Identify realistic functionality and build a minimum proof-of-concept for RTGS system on DLT platform	Ethereum
Phase 2	Nov. 2016	1. Analyse competing blockchain platforms using the selected use case as a benchmark 2. Address the privacy issues identified in the previous phase	Corda

Fig 8.8-1: CBDC Projects across the world (www.bot.or.th/)

European Central Bank & Bank of Japan		Project Stella	
Phase 1	May. 2017	1 Build RTGS system on DLT, including LSM functions 2 Assess safety and efficiency of current system in DLT implementation	Hyperledger Fabric
Phase 2	Nov. 2017	1 Build DvP proof-of-concept on different DLT platforms 2 Identify the trade-off between network size and performance 3 Assess DLT capability for cross-chain securities settlement	Quorum, Corda, Hyperledger Fabric, Elements
Hong Kong Monetary Authority		Project Lionrock	
Phase 1	Aug. 2016	1 Identify use cases and build a working prototype for the central bank using DLT 2 Identify realistic functionality and build a minimum proof-of concept for RTGS system on DLT platform	Corda
South African Reserve Bank		Project Khokha	
Phase 1	Feb. 2018	1 Build an RTGS proof-of-concept on DLT, exploring on privacy and scalability 2 Perform tests under a variety of deployment models in different locations 3 Assess a Quorum-based interbank payment system	Quorum

Fig 8.8-2: CBDC Projects across the world -2

(Fig 4.10 https://www.bot.or.th/)

Case Study: Central Bank Digital Currency experiment by Bank of Thailand (Project Inthanon) https://www.bot.or.th/English/FinancialMarkets/ProjectInthanon/Documents/Inthanon_Phase2_Report.pdf

Project Inthanon was devided into three progressive phases, each leveraging on the findings and learnings of the previous phase

01 **Phase 1 – Building the Fundamental**

A POC for a DLT-based RTGS using wholesale CBDC for interbank settlement was built. A key highlight was the development of an innovative QR architecture with integrated Automated Liquidity Provision (ALP) functionality that achieved privacy and atomicity properties.

02 **Phase 2 – Enhancing Functionalities**

The objective is to build on the Phase 1 POC and augment it with additional functions to handle DvP settlement for interbank bond repo & trading, data reconciliation and handling of RR regulatory requirements. Outcomes from Phase 2 demonstrate the practicality of DLT at enabling transformative process improvement and technical feasibility of achieving DvP in real-time through an experimental MLSM.

03 **Phase 3 – Exploring Cross-Border Funds Transfer Models**

The DLT-based RTGS prototype will be expanded to connect with the other systems to support cross-border funds transfer transactions. The scope will also cover the regulatory and compliance issues from both THB and foreign currencies.

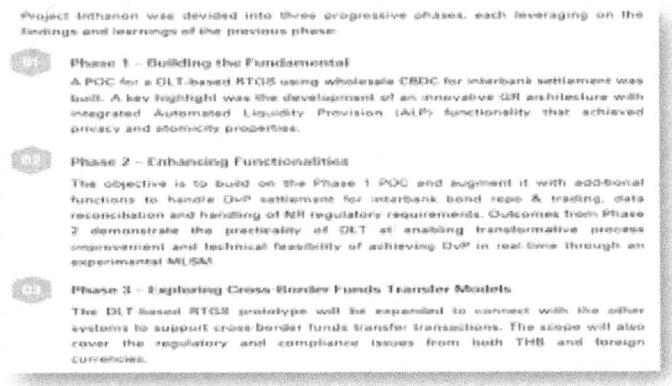

Fig 8.8-3: CBDC & Financial Assets on Blockchain Project Inathon by Thailand Government

Bank of Thailand completed Phase-1 and Phase-2 successfully and has demonstrated many advantages of issuing the Central Bank-backed digital currencies over a Distributed ledger.

The findings from Phase-2 demonstrated the feasibility of Smart Contract utilization to automate bond life cycle events and DvP (Delivery Versus Payment) of inter-bank bond trading and repo transactions. The effective use of Smart Contracts has shown the potential to significantly streamline operational workflows and increase efficiencies. Fraud-prevention capabilities of the RTGS system were also augmented by the creation of a new end-to-end workflow that allowed validation of transactional information with external sources through integration points. The use of Smart Contracts for regulatory compliance purposes was also successfully tested in Phase-2 with the introduction of the NRFS mechanism, which could potentially
eliminate multiple manual operational processes and allow banks to monitor NRBA/ NRBS limits more effectively.

Land Titling using Blockchain in Smart Cities

A number of leading Digital Nations like UK, Dubai, Sweden have already started using Blockchain for maintaining Land Records, following case study of Land Pooling in APCRDA (Andhra Pradesh Capital Region Development Authority) elucidates how developing countries which are plagued by frauds and court cases in their Land Registry system can leverage Blockchain. Final implementation is however a long-drawn-out process involving multiple interactions, government transitions and resistance to change that could derail the process.

Case study of APCRDA for Blockchain in Land Pooling & Land Titling (Source: AP Govt records in public domain) is discussed here.

Background:

When a new city is developed from the scratch, land has to be pooled from existing owners and redistributed. In this process, the land parcels owned by individuals or group of owners are legally consolidated by transfer of ownership rights to the authority. It later transfers the ownership of a part of land back to the landowners for undertaking of development of such areas. In LPS the landowner will be getting Returnable Plots for the land he has surrendered with consent.

Implementation Process:

Blockchain solution integrates with existing department systems through API calls & coexists non intrusively.

●● Uses http API calls – can integrate with systems/GIS Systems on different technical platforms.

●● APCRDA GIS System data (Land Information) has been stored in Blockchain in Geo-json format.

●● Modifications/Alterations of land records to follow the approved process and option is given for Authenticated Users only.

●● Upon User request, GIS System (ArcGIS Server) generates Parcel images (Parcel, Block & Colony level location maps) along with Coordinates and Centroid of Parcel for Registration.

●● Request API at Block chain server generates Block Chain Certificate embedded with QR Code (Information of Property).

●● Existing systems include all transaction validation

business logic & call APIs of Blockchain for respective data

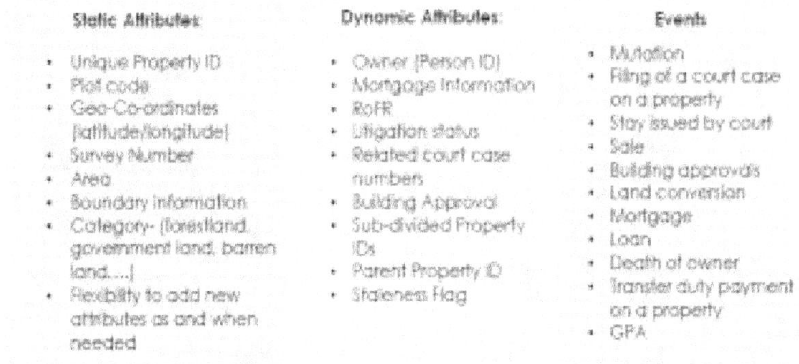

Static Attributes:
• Unique Property ID
• Plot code
• Geo-Co-ordinates (latitude/longitude)
• Survey Number
• Area
• Boundary information
• Category- (forestland, government land, barren land....)
• Flexibility to add new attributes as and when needed
Dynamic Attributes:
• Owner (Person ID)
• Mortgage Information
• RoFR
• Litigation status
• Related court case numbers
• Building Approval
• Sub-divided Property IDs
• Parent Property ID
• Staleness Flag
Events:
• Mutation
• Filing of a court case on a property
• Stay issued by court
• Sale
• Building approvals
• Land conversion
• Mortgage
• Loan
• Death of owner
• Transfer duty payment on a property
• GPA

Fig 8.9: Details recorded on Blockchain with timestamps

The details recorded chronologically and queryable using the Blockchain explorer are given in the following:

- Mutation
- Filing of a court case on a property
- Stay by court
- Sale
- Building Construction approvals
- Land conversion
- Mortgage
- Loan
- Death of owner
- Transfer duty paid on a property
- GPA

Solution Architecture:

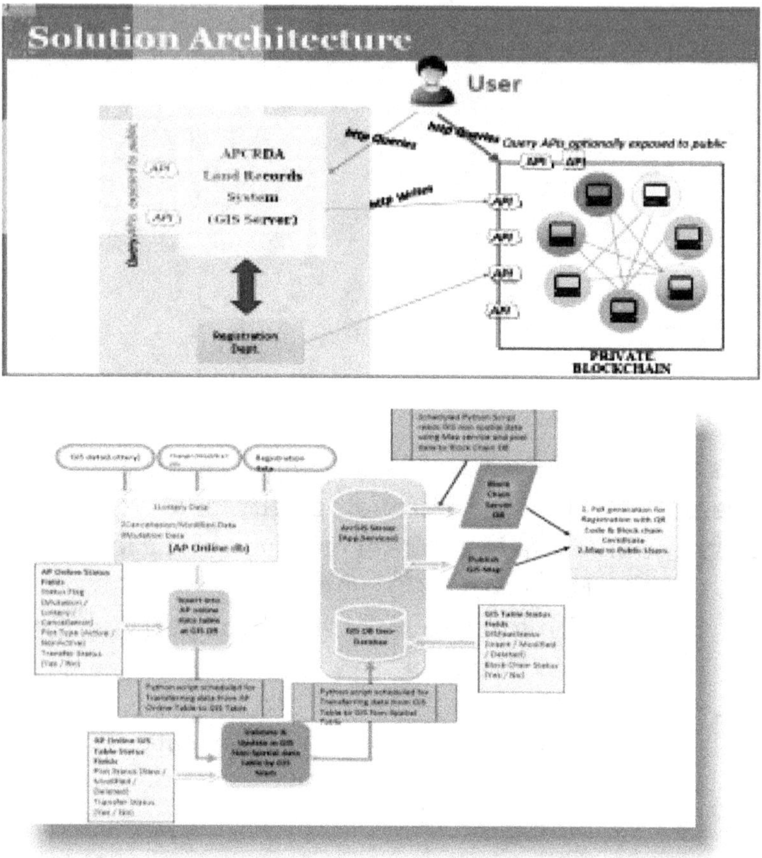

Fig 8.10-1,2: APCRDA Land Record Blockchain application Solution Architecture

Blockchain based Property certificate is issued to the owners and verifiable for authenticity on Blockchain.

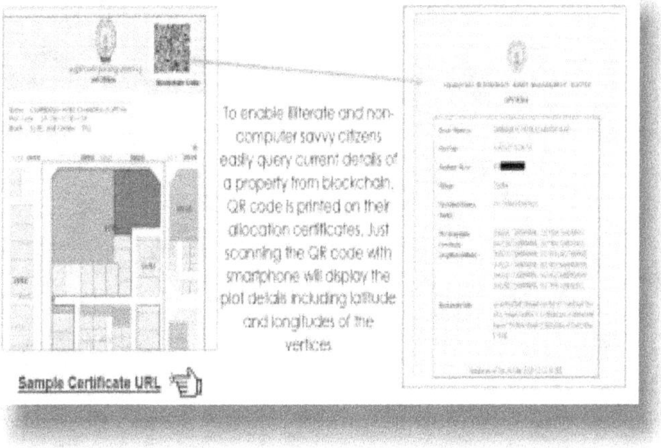

Fig 8.10-3: Blockchain based QR code embedded Land ownership document

The benefits of the project are summarised below:

- All property record creation and changes are entered into the immutable ledger along with digital signatures of the authorized officers. Due to cumulative hashing even super-users cannot tamper the data & QR code-based property ownership Blockchain Certificates are provided to citizens.

- Geo-fencing capability to identify overlaps across plots.
- Capability to integrate with property tax system to enable simple, efficient and transparent record of ownership and tax transactions on a given property.

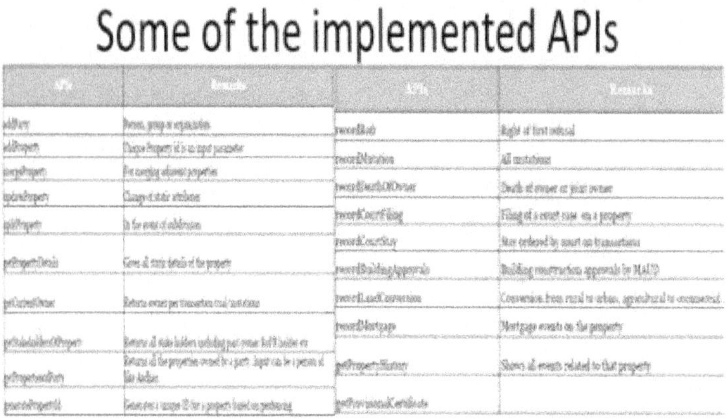

Fig 8.11: APIs implemented for interaction with Blockchain

- Capability for instant data exchange through Smart Contract powered Data-as-a-Service (DaaS) leading to additional revenue to the Government through exposed APIs.
- API calls with banks and financial institutions for quick and secure execution of loans and sale transactions.

Blockchain and Sustainable Development Goals (SDG)

The Sustainable Development Goals are a collection of 17 global goals designed to be a "blueprint to achieve a better and more sustainable future for all."

The SDGs, set in 2015 by the United Nations General Assembly and intended to be achieved by the year 2030, are part of UN Resolution 70/1, the 2030 Agenda. (Wikipedia)

Fig 8.12 Sustainable Development Goals:
Source: https://sustainabledevelopment.un.org/sdgs

Blockchain has helped in a multipronged approach to attain the Sustainable Development Goals by all nations. The utility of Blockchain for the same is given as follows.

1. Eliminate Poverty: Targeted Govt. benefits to poor persons with no leakages.
2. Eliminate Hunger: Support Humanitarian activities targeted at food distribution in a coordinated manner. Crowdsource and track information on people deprived of daily minimum needs for ex. World Food Program.
3. Good health and well-being: Track medical records, eliminate fake drugs, support clinical trials and Pharma research and deliver and monitor high-quality subsidized cheap drugs. Track immunization health records of children through their early life. Insurance for all, especially pregnant women, elderly, poor and vulnerable tracked through Blockchain.
4. Quality education: Track academic credentials on Blockchain and support brilliant and downtrodden through scholarships and the right opportunities for global exposure of talent of them and to them.
5. Gender Equality: Incentivize and reward organiza-

tions and regions showing better performance on gender parity in areas like board rooms, staff ratio and Woman safety. Offer a channel for new employment opportunities for women with career breaks and with handicaps. Track safety measures and actions against atrocities for women in a coordinated manner.

6. Clean water and sanitation: Tracking effluents of industry, water pollution levels of major river bodies, the health of lakes, utilization of budgets targeted for Water conservation, Rainwater harvesting track records and efforts, etc.

7. Clean renewable energy: Enable peer-to-peer renewable energy trading, Reward renewable energy consumption, Track carbon certificates, facilitate measurement of usage and generation.

8. Sustainable employment: Verified expertise credentials and facilitate the gig economy for trusted peer-to-peer project marketplace

9. Innovation, industrialization, and infrastructure: Protect patents and help share and monetize intellectual capital. 3Dmanufacturing for productive industries and fast deployments, encourage recycling and reuse of industrial waste and residue.

10. Reduce country-level inequalities: Cross-country global cooperation, resource trading with reduced costs and complexities.

11. Safe Smart Cities: Secure IOT infrastructure with Blockchain for scalable automation.

12. Responsible Production and consumption: Tracking supply chains for ethical sourcing and providing live accurate data for forecasting.

13. Climate action: Track and reward environment conservation actions and progressive improvements across

regions for reducing pollution.
14. Life underwater: Track the quality of seawater for harmful effluents and take steps to address deteriorations.
15. Life on land: Track forest fires on live basis across the world, take steps to track and improve afforestation, check desertification, aid in disaster management activities through coordinated actions.
16. Peace, Justice and Strong Institutions: ID2020 and Digital Identities. Blockchains enable trust which would, in turn, help mitigate corruption.
17. Partnerships: Global partnerships with win-win associations with collaboration, coordination, communication, cooperation facilitated by Blockchain.
Thus, Blockchain has significant applications in Smart city Projects and in achieving Sustainable Development Goals as laid down by United Nations.

In India, Government of India subsidises the pricing of fertilisers sold to farmers. The difference between the sale price and the certified cost price is passed as a credit to the fertiliser manufacturers by the Government.
Due to a vast number of intermediaries, need for a lot of documentation, certifications and associated trust requirement and complexity, there is a significant delay in the processing of the subsidies leading to wastage of costs connected with accounting, documentation, intermediaries and reconciliation.
Niti Aayog in association with PwC, a global leading consulting firm and Intel to conceive and implement a Blockchain pilot project to solve the above problems by leveraging its trusted automation capability.
The following figure depicts the details of the pilot implemented.

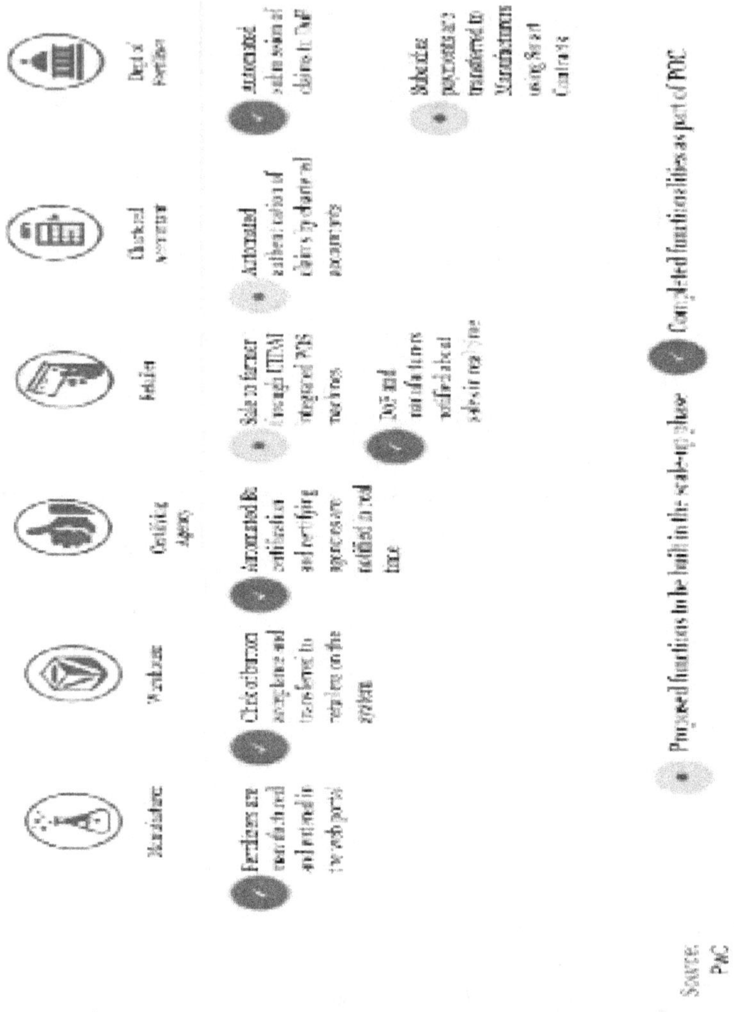

Fig 8.13: Blockchain pilot for Subsidy transfer Source: Niti Aayog Blockchain strategy report (Use case in collaboration with PwC)

The following benefits have been realised due to the implementation of Blockchain solution.

1. Productivity increase: Substantial reduction time taken for transaction acknowledgements between multiple parties involved.

2. Near real time B1 certification: Immediate reporting

of the details of the shipments against a few weeks taken earlier for reporting the same.

3. Eliminated paper trails – Elimination of vast amount of paperwork and replacing the same with digital trails thus reducing a lot of cost.

4. Standardised documents & easy entries: The use of standardised document templates & agreement templates eliminated need for associated clerical time.

Eliminating Fake drug menace:

A lot of lives across the world are lost due to the consumption of fake pharmaceutical drugs.

NITI Aayog, along with a global pharmaceutical giant and other leading health care value chain participants, joined hands with Oracle to implement a pilot project to track and trace the pharmaceutical drugs from the manufacturer to the final chemist outlet. The details of the same are depicted in the following diagram.

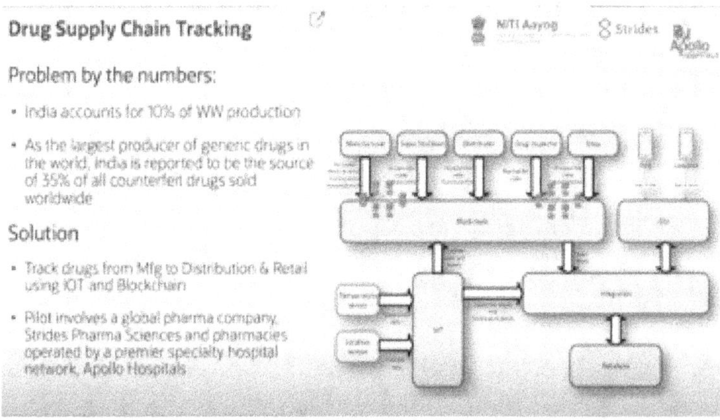

Fig 8.14: Blockchain, IoT, Cloud integration for medicinal drug traceability

The following benefits were realised due to the Blockchain implementation:

End to end traceability of Pharmaceutical drugs for all

stakeholders.
Any Problems could be traced to the origin of the incidence increasing accountability.
Medicine could be located with precision to ensure delivery planning and follow up.
A common Blockchain platform implementation could eliminate the fake drug menace.

Blockchain based Academic Certificates:
Problem:
As we have seen in the earlier sections, the paper- based certificates used by various academic institution need to be verified for authenticity at various junctures of a students' career and there are prone to not only duplication or fakes, but also to substantial verification process delays.
To overcome this problem, Niti Aayog evaluated the concept of issuing Blockchain based academic certificates, that are instantly and authentically verified from anywhere in the world.
The following process depicts the use of Blockchain to issue instantly verifiable certificates.

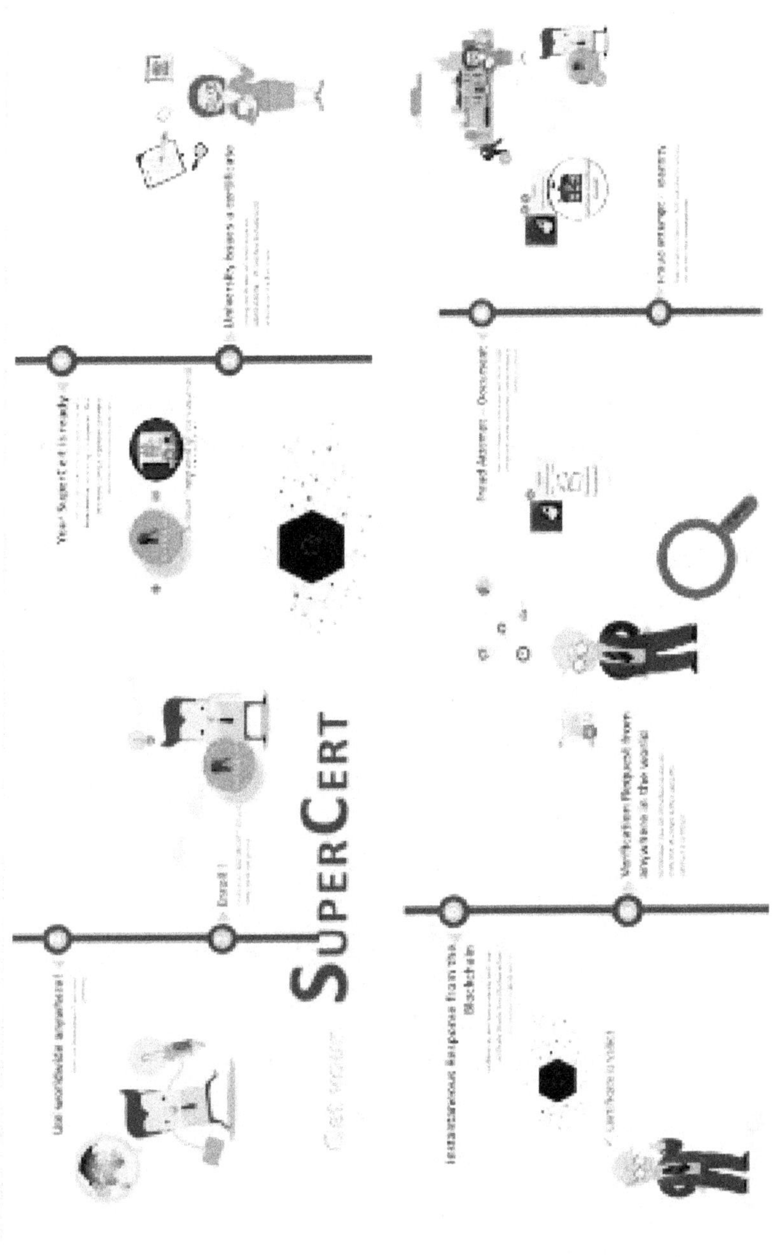

Fig 8.15: Blockchain based academic certificates (NITI

Aayog, ISB)

The following benefits have been understood from the analysis of the Blockchain SuperCert project.
i. Data privacy: data stays with the entities that own them.
ii. Real-time, automated verification from anywhere in the world.
iii. Tamper and fraud resistant – Not possible for anyone to tamper with the certification contents.
iv. Permanence: the certificates will survive beyond organisations – removes dependence on the issuing authority for future verifications.
v. Scalable to national and global level- The system eliminates manual record keeping and transportation of paper documents across the world, thus allowing form scalable automation.

Niti Aayog's paper demonstrates many more such real-life examples that includes use cases like:

- Secure personal document digital vault.
- Vaccine supply chain tracking.
- Trusted administration of Chit-fund transactions.
- Insurance (Medical, Automotive, etc.)
- EV Battery Swapping
- Organic Farming
- Energy management etc.

For more detailed understanding of these case studies, please refer to the document at

https://niti.gov.in/sites/default/files/2020-01/Blockchain_The_India_Strategy_Part_I.pdf

The use of Blockchain technology helps in the following

aspects:

- Reduction in transaction costs due to elimination of non-value adding middlemen.
- Trust through the Blockchain system as all transactions are recorded on a distributed ledger with established identities and are time stamped.
- Transparency and elimination of duplicity or mistakes in invoices as all records are managed through a streamlined process and verified formats that are encoded into the system.
- All parties can operate in a safe and efficient environment, devoid of human dependency.

It is imperative that Blockchain applications fall within the realm of laws of the land to be able to win the confidence and support of the regulators and the government authorities, without which these applications are doomed to fail.

The central question is not how to regulate Blockchains, but how Blockchains regulate. They may supplement, complement, or substitute existing structures for legal enforcement. Excessive or premature application of rigid legal obligations will stymie innovation and forego opportunities to leverage technology to achieve public policy objectives. Blockchain developers and legal institutions can work together. Each must recognize the unique affordances of the other system. (Reference: Trust, But Verify: Why the Blockchain Needs the Law: Kevin Werbach, University of Pennsylvania, The Wharton School, Legal Studies & Business Ethics Department).

While applications that leverage Blockchain as a Supplement or a Complement for legal enforcement, any application that is seen as a substitute for legal enforcement by offering a radically different approach to governance like bitcoin or the decentralised autonomous organisations are seen to be too radical and will not find favour with the regulators and will not survive in the long run.

Noteworthy non-finance applications on Blockchain globally

Project No	Project Name	Country of implementation	Field of implementation	Level of government involved
1	Exonum land title registry	Georgia	Land title registry; property transactions	National
2	Blockcerts academic credentials	Malta	Academic certificates verification; personal documents storage and sharing	National
3	Chromaway property transactions	Sweden	Property transactions; transfer of land titles	National
4	uPort decentralised identity	Switzerland	Digital identity for proof of residency, eVoting, payments for bike rental and parking	Local (Municipality of Zug)
5	Infrachain governance framework	Luxemburg	Blockchain governance	National
6	Pension infrastructure	The Netherlands	Pension system management	National
7	Stadjerspas smart vouchers	The Netherlands	Benefit management for low-income residents	Local (Municipality of Groningen)

Fig 8.16: Noteworthy Global Blockchain Govt Applications

Source: Blockchain for Digital Governments, An assessment of pioneering implementations. A report by JRC Science for Policy report by European Commission

In May 2015, NASDAQ announced that it sees, the Blockchain as providing "extensive integrity, audit ability, governance and transfer of ownership capabilities". As reflected in the above table, Blockchain has been seen to have extensive applications in the following areas:

- KYC, Identity & Access management,
- Verifiable claims of ownership of certificates ranging from academic to asset ownership and variety of other certificates,
- Auditable track and trace record in the supply chains, transfer of ownership & invoice financing,
- Registry of Land registries, medical records, birth and death certificates
- Financial applications like cross border & inter-bank money transfers, insurance claim settlement, commercial paper issuances, loan account management etc.
- Lot security and smart contract settlements in derivate trading
- Cross enterprise collaboration in finance, supply chain, agriculture, energy trading and healthcare domains

We expect all these applications to flourish by leveraging a combination of a Permissioned Private or Consortium Blockchain with hashes recorded and anchored on Public Permissioned Blockchain launched by the Government of India.

1. Blockchain Triggered Opportunity for India

India is a country with over 1.3 billion citizens, and a huge concentration of smartphones. With 1.21 billion mobile connections, 1.19 billion Aadhaar enrolments, 462 million Internet users, 582 million bank accounts and 375 million social media users, India is one of the largest generators of online data globally.

Monetising data being generated by its citizens and billions of Internet of Things (IoT) devices in the future in a secure and anonymised manner made possible by Blockchain, has the potential to catapult India to one of the richest countries in the world in future.

Apart from existing connections, the increase in the number of IoT devices will lead to a huge deluge of data. Unlocking the value of the data in the hands of citizens in a secure manner could give a big boost to citizens' disposable incomes. This implies an urgent need to set up a trusted and centralised data repository, and a mechanism to enable citizens and organisations to monetise the data in a secure and credible manner.

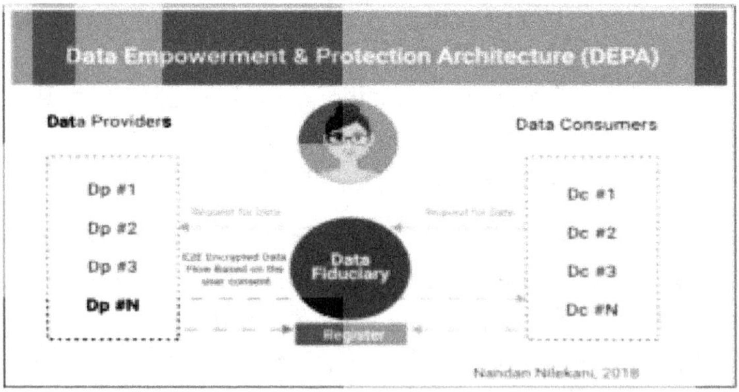

Fig 8.17: Trusted Data exchange between Parties (Courtesy: Nandan Nilekani)

Currently, a lot of organisations like ecommerce companies, banks, NBFCs, telecom companies, employment exchanges etc., are sitting on a vast amount of data which they mine using advanced analytics to increase the lifetime value of their customers. To enable them to target a greater number of customers effectively, and increase their business, they need to exchange and procure data from other sources and organisations. This calls for a mechanism to exchange curated data among holders of the data across organisations and individuals. This can be made possible with Blockchain. For this, a normalising means for commercial exchange is needed, which can be made possible with a data token on a Blockchain system.

This will have implications for all sectors of the economy as a trusted data source at a nominal cost will be available for sectors like education, healthcare, telecom, NBFCs and banks. Interestingly, across the world, there are a number of companies leveraging Blockchain technologies to forge commercial interactions between data generating and data seeking organisations.

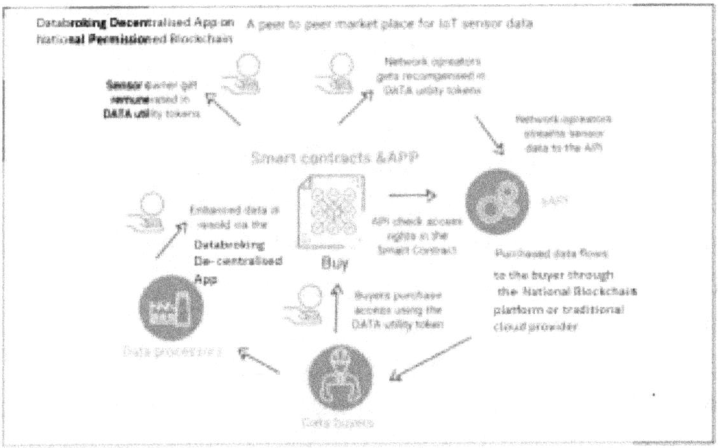

Fig 8.18: Data Broker platform on a DLT to unlock the value of Data

2. Central Bank Digital currency on a Permissioned Ledger

As an alternative to Public Blockchains that operate with native cryptocurrency, like Ethereum, it is strongly recommended that Government of India along with RBI come out with a Central Bank Digital INR (CBDR) administered over a Public Permissioned Blockchain that processes transactions through a Turing Complete Virtual Machine allowing decentralised applications to run on its platform.

Central bank digital currency (CBDC), also called digital fiat currency or digital base money is the digital form of fiat money (a currency established as money by government regulation or law). Central bank digital currency is different from virtual currency and cryptocurrency, which are not issued by the state and lack the legal tender status declared by the government.

The advantage of offering CBDR is that it can allow the Indian Blockchain developers and entrepreneurs to create and run decentralised applications like in the case of the open source Permissionless Blockchains like Ethereum, EOS etc., while benefiting from regulatory oversight and corresponding protection.

A number of countries in the world are experimenting with the concept of CBDC and it is considered a transitory step to the ultimate eventuality of a fully digitalised currency with the added security measure offered by a Blockchain approach.

Globally many Blockchain applications employ a 'Hybrid' approach where a combination of private and public Blockchain systems is used to secure the integrity of

the data stored. A case in point is the land registry application by the National Agency of Public Registry (NAPR) of the Republic of Georgia which uses Blockchain as shown in the figure below:
Instead of the Bitcoin Blockchain in the below example, we propose that similar applications can use to anchor their hashes on a Public Permissioned Blockchain created by Government of India and RBI that also are powered by a CBDR on the ledger.

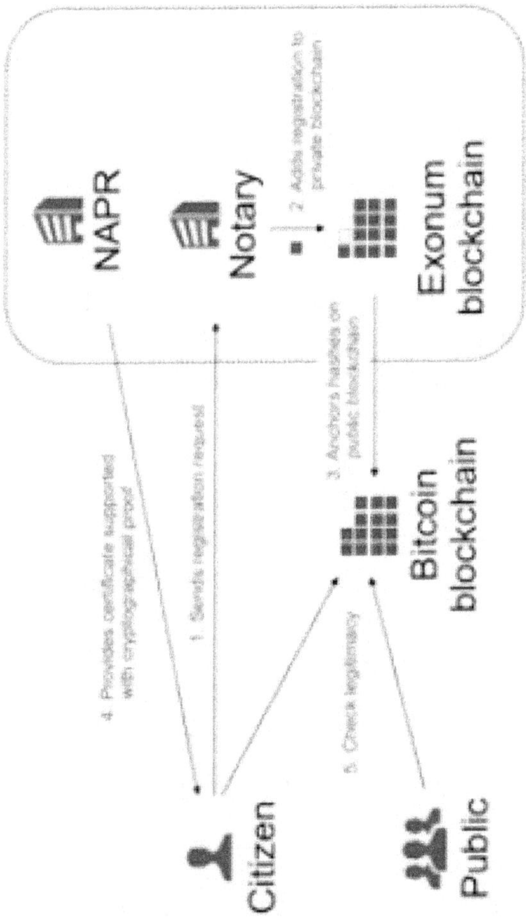

Fig 8.19: Hybrid Blockchain Application for Land Registry by Government of Malta

Source: Blockchain for Digital Governments, An assessment of pioneering implementations. A report by JRC Science for Policy report by European Commission

The National Permissioned Blockchain can offer 'Trust as a Service' to a variety of decentralised applications and any number of permissioned Blockchain applications as depicted in the above example.

An option for technical implementation of the National Public Blockchain could be a Quorum or a Private Ethereum version with a Proof of Authority Consensus Mechanism, with the validator nodes being hosted by selected Government departments and Industry Associations. There can be many other options that need to be evaluated before a final decision is taken by the Government in this regard.

By undertaking these actions, Government of India can send a strong signal about its intention to leverage Blockchain technology and facilitate a vibrant industry and start-up ecosystem that caters to the demand of all industries - public and private. This will institutionalise Blockchain applications, while availing the Trust as a Service facility of the Public Permissioned Blockchain network under the aegis of various Indian regulators. The decentralised applications that can be created over this network can also facilitate India's participation in the Industry 4.0 revolution through scalable & secure automation. The monetary value of the data expected to be generated by IoT devices can be unlocked bringing prosperity to India and its citizens.

Having made Proof of Concepts, a number of Blockchain

companies and start-ups across India, await a clear direction and policy from Government to go to the next level of implementing such projects on a large scale to derive the full benefits of this amazing technology paradigm through improved Governance.

CHAPTER 9: BLOCKCHAIN COUNTRIES

Distributed ledger technology overcomes the problems of data centralisation thus, de-risking with respect to ransomware while overcoming limitations due to imperfect information infrastructure.

2. Real time sharing of data across participants is made possible thus unifying the data silos.

3. Immutable and tamper features of blockchain can improve trust, increase transparency & efficiency for a better cooperation & collaboration between departments.

4. Smart contract-based transactions will dramatically improve scalability of transactions at the same time eliminating unwanted human interference. This offers immense flexibility for smart cities and makes them viable.

Some case studies of Blockchain application in different countries across the world are given as follow:

1. China

China is home to some of the largest number of Blockchain projects with the Government encouraging the companies and start-ups to actively create innovative Blockchain applications to eliminate corruption and increase transparency in transactions.

While it is not considered illegal to buy, sell or hold Bitcoins and other cryptocurrencies the Chinese government encourages only those Blockchain activities that service the real economy.

Chinese Government launched BSN (Blockchain based Services Network), an information infrastructure where all members share the same public services provided by their Government. The network aims to provide a unique global public infrastructure network in order to accelerate digital commerce.

Think of it like an operating system, where participants can use existing blockchain programs, or build their own bespoke tools, without having to design a framework from the ground up.

The BSN's proponents say it will reduce the costs of doing blockchain-based business by 80 percent. By the end of 2020, they hope to have nodes in 200 Chinese cities. Eventually, they believe it could become a global standard.

China leads the world in blockchain-related patents, according to the World Intellectual Property Organization. And blockchain goes far beyond Bitcoin; the technology can be used to verify all sorts of transactions (Source IEEE)

Case 1: China Transportation Chain:

Launched by Ministry of Transport & 5 companies in city of Wuxi to solve problems of:

1. Traffic Congestion through better information sharing,
2. Construction of urban parking facilities,
3. Penalties for traffic violations, and
4. Information security of the Internet of Vehicles.

Case 2: Carbon Bank (Automobile) Public Chain Platform:

BYD (Carbon Bank integration platform), DNV GL (Certification), Veechain (Blockchain platform for automotive lifecycle management) are collaborating to integrate information of cars, large passenger cars,
and other vehicles for on-chain storage.

Dubai

Dubai is patronizing Blockchain to eliminate all paper records across its governance, land records management, Police evidence tracking, Passport and VISA tracking, Cross/border remittances,
Citizen Medical records tracking, etc., and save 5.5 billion dirhams annually in document processing alone equal to the one Burj Khalifa's worth of value every year. Giving itself an ambitious target of becoming a paperless country, Dubai Government has been pioneering Blockchain and emerging technologies through a series of measures.
Dubai Land Department is employing the Blockchain in three initiatives (Ownership verification in DLD Mobile Application, Property sale by Developer and Smart Leasing Process) targeting the improvement of providing the services, improve the collaboration with other parties involved the real estate market and to create a secured digital assets A sample copy of a Land deed digitised on a Blockchain is given in the following figure.

Fig 9.1 Blockchain record of a Land title deed in Dubai

Further, Dubai is one of the leading exponents of all emerging technologies. Status of some of the Blockchain initiatives in Dubai are summarised in the following figure:

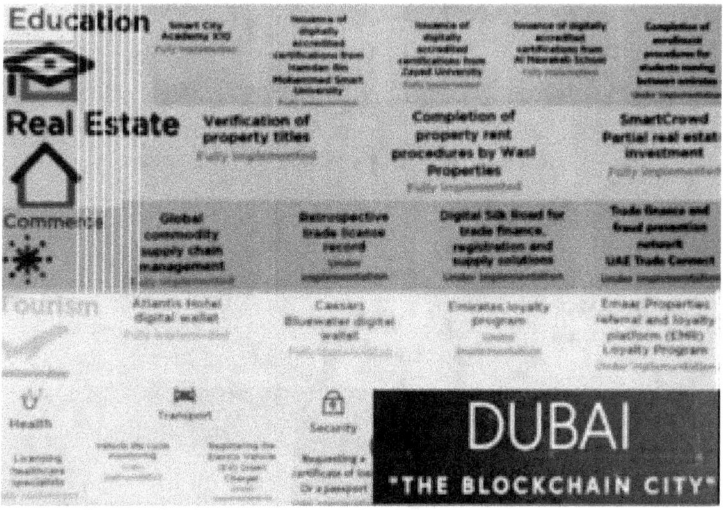

Fig 9.2: Blockchain projects being implemented with encouragement from Dubai Govt.

ESTONIA:

Estonia a small country with 1.3 million population and an erstwhile part of Soviet Union, is extensively using Blockchain for the Integrity of data pertaining to all public and citizen records, Critical Infrastructure Protection and Secured access of all Government services to citizens through a Blockchain enabled digital identity. Estonia uses one of the most advanced Digital Citizen Identity management system.

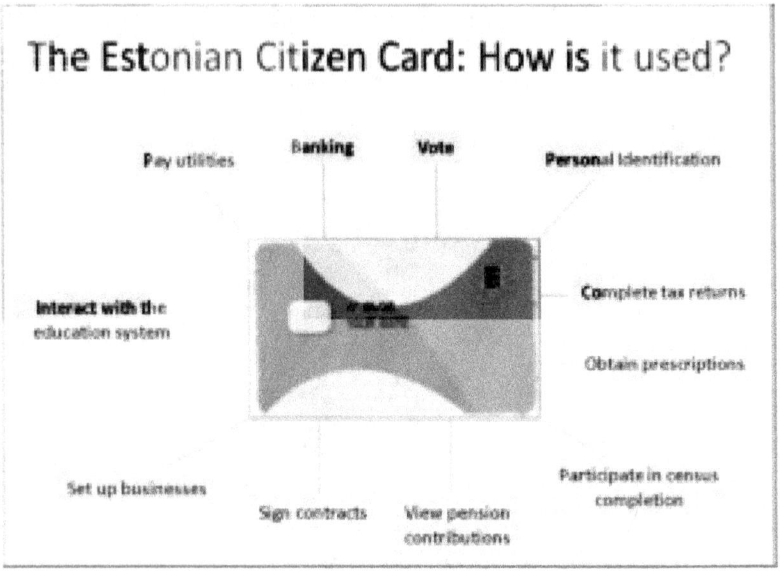

Fig 9.3:Estonia's Citizen identity card (Source: Estonia Govt. portal)

Estonia secured all its citizens' medical records on a Blockchain. Estonia leverages KSI Blockchain technology to secure the Electronic Health Records (e-Health Record) of its 1.3 million citizens.

Fig 9.4: Estonia's integrated Blockchain platform to access citizen services. Source: Estonia Govt records in public domain

The Integrated Blockchain platform implemented by Estonia offers the following:

1. 100% of citizen data secured on Blockchain and offers an integrity layer across all the Government departments.
2. Data across all the departments segregated for privacy & confidentiality but unified to integrate silos for de-duplication.
3. Complete transparency and accountability between citizens and their governments.
4. Blockchain protects the data across various G2C services cutting across various departments like Health, Education, Law & Order, Agriculture, Revenue & Land records, Corporate affairs etc.

The e-Health Record system offers an integrated view of the patient's records, test results including image files such as X-Rays issued by different hospitals and laboratories. The integrity of the records is ensured by the Blockchain while the doctors can get a complete view of the medical history of their patients via the e-Patient portal.

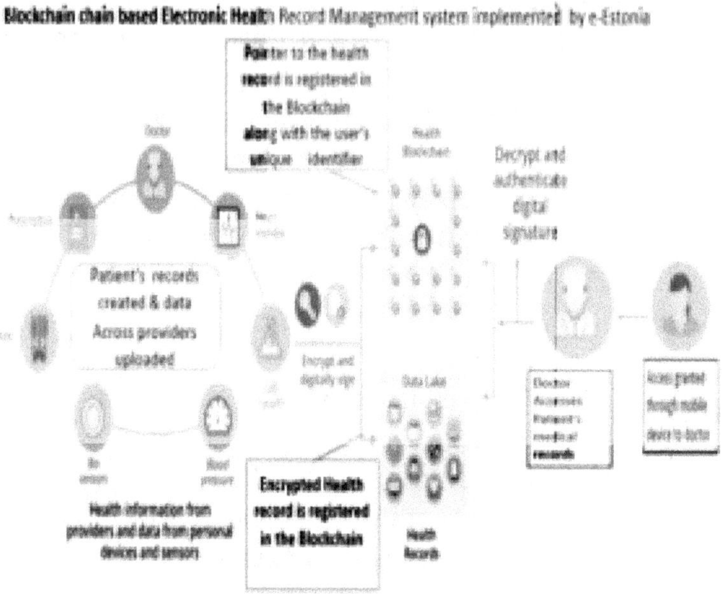

Fig 9.5: Integrated e-Health Record System of e-Estonia

The patients can have a complete record of their reports, transactions and doctor access and comments, maintain privacy and secrecy of their information while getting an integrated view of their personal records as per the access privileges built in.

European Union: European Blockchain services infrastructure project, EBSI, was launched by the European Union enables users to store and transmit data in a secure, decentralized manner and deliver better services to Europe's citizens.

India

India's Telecom Regulatory Authority is using Distributed Ledger Technology for tracking Unsolicited Commercial Communication. Several states, Ministries, Income Tax department, Customs department, Public Sector Undertakings, NPCI and Police departments are vigorously exploring Blockchain to improve transparency, efficiency and eliminate corruption and fake products, documents, identity, and certificates menace.

Popular Use cases in India
1. Academic Certificates For instant Verification from anywhere
2. Benefit Distribution- Direct transfer to deserving beneficiaries
3. Clearing and Settlement – Vajra Platform by NPCI
4. Distribution & Container Supply chain- Adani Ports & TradeLens
5. Electronic Procurement Management – Minimise middlemen and Transparent bid management
6. Farm to fork supply chain for transparency, efficiency & disintermediation
7. GI Tags for Authentic Organic and Premium product manufactures
8. Income Tax Department – Income and Tax verification for loan and deposit applicants
9. Land Records- To authenticate Land ownerships & eliminate disputes
10. Tool Life cycle tracking & management in Manufacturing plants
TRAI - For blocking UCC (Unsolicited Commercial Communication)
Other Applications working on Leveraging Distributed Ledge Technology:
Digital Identity, Central Bank Digital Currency, Compliance tracking, Voting , Secure Data Vault

Fig 9.6: Popular Use cases in India

Singapore:

Singapore is working on a Blockchain-based payment system using digital Singapore Dollars, that can be used to execute inter-bank and cross currency remittances quickly and affordably and with fewer intermediaries. Being a global hub for Finance and Supply Chain activities and organizations, Singapore Government enables a vibrant Blockchain ecosystem for enterprises to experiment and implement entire spectrum of Permissioned and Permissionless Blockchain applications across Finance, Supply Chain, trade finance, Crowdfunding, health insurance, Digital SGD, Academic certificates, etc.

MAS is taking an active role in experimenting with

disruptive technologies like Blockchain, where it is adopting a five phased approach of moving the killer applications like Cross Border Trade and currency exchange from idea stage to production stage. MAS began experimenting with Blockchain by launching Project UBIN, to digitise Singapore Dollar and use a DLT ledger to transfer these Digital dollars across the banks in the country. After successful experimentation it has now cleared multiple stages of evolution

to now be ready to adopt this technology for a number of use cases like Cross border remittances, connecting Singapore exchange with global trade and financial ecosystems, trade network exchanges for leveraging Distributed ledger technology for instant clearing and settlement.

PROJECT UBIN PHASE (1 – 5) by Monetary Authority of Singapore's Project for evaluating applications of Blockchain for clearing and settlement in Cross Border Trade, across Currencies

Courtesy: The Monetary Authority of Singapore (MAS) and Temasek report "Project Ubin Phase 5: Enabling Broad Ecosystem Opportunities".

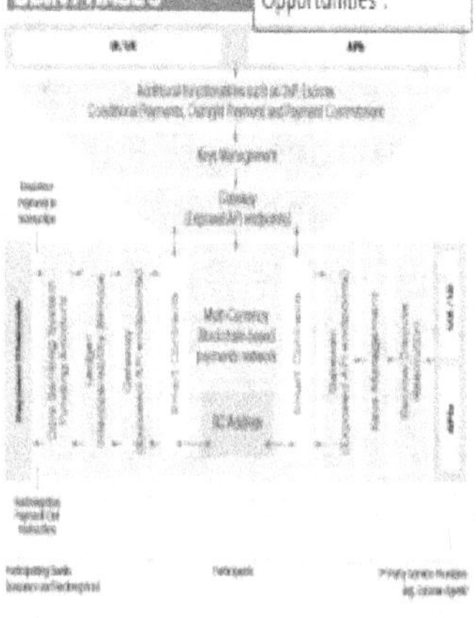

Project Ubin is a collaborative project with the industry to explore the use of blockchain and distributed ledger technology for the clearing and settlement of payments and securities with a goal to develop simpler-to-use and more efficient alternatives to today's systems, and that are based on central bank-issued digital tokens.

Phase 1 MAS, R3 & consortium of financial institutions on a PoC to conduct inter-bank payments using blockchain technology.

Phase 2 MAS and the Association of Banks in Singapore (ABS) led the successful development of software prototypes of three different models for decentralised inter-bank payments and settlements with liquidity savings mechanisms..

Phase 3: Delivery versus Payment (DvP) MAS and Singapore Exchange (SGX) collaborated to develop Delivery versus Payment (DvP) capabilities for settlement of tokenised assets across different blockchain platforms, and defined a market framework that governs post-trade settlement processes such as arbitration.

Phase 4: Cross-border Payment versus Payment (PvP) The Bank of Canada (BoC), linked up their respective experimental domestic payment networks, namely Project Ubin and Project Jasper, and conducted a successful experiment on cross-border and cross-currency payments using central bank digital currencies.

Phase 5: Enabling Broad Ecosystem Opportunities , the final phase developed the multi-currency payments model described in Phase 4, conducted connectivity testing with other blockchain applications & proved the business value of a blockchain-based payments network.

Fig 9.7 5 stages of Project UBIN by Monetary Authorities of Singapore

United Kingdom

UK Government has been exploring Blockchain for several use cases like Central Bank Digital Currency for instant Inter-bank remittances, clearing and settlement, land records management,

Government Data Provenance, Voting, Benefit and Charity distribution and Food safety in Supply Chains.

10. USA: US Government is working extensively on several Blockchain projects in Pharmaceuticals, Food, Cannabis, Defence Supply Chain provenance, health record tracking, Clinical records management, etc. Department of Homeland Security is researching Blockchain extensively for Critical

Infrastructure protection using Blockchain enabled identification systems.

Thailand: Thailand Government is extensively experimenting with Blockchain for a variety of applications involving Digital identity, Supply chain and Central Bank Digital currencies. Case study of Thailand Government's initiatives in Blockchain are covered in Annexure 1.

CHAPTER 10: CHALLENGES AND LIMITATIONS OF IMPLEMENTING BLOCKCHAIN SOLUTIONS

Governments across the world have accelerated their adoption of Blockchain applications for transforming their citizen services.

Different Governments are at different stages of adoption. We have seen Governments launch their strategy and approach papers.

As discussed in Chapter 2, there are a number of key benefits sought after by them to transform their working and present substantial convenience, transparency to their citizens. Blockchain being still in its early stage of evolution, a lot of developments that take place across the nook and corners of the world are seeking to mitigate these challenges as we go along.

Some of the challenges that we face in implementing the Blockchain based applications are summarised in the following figure:

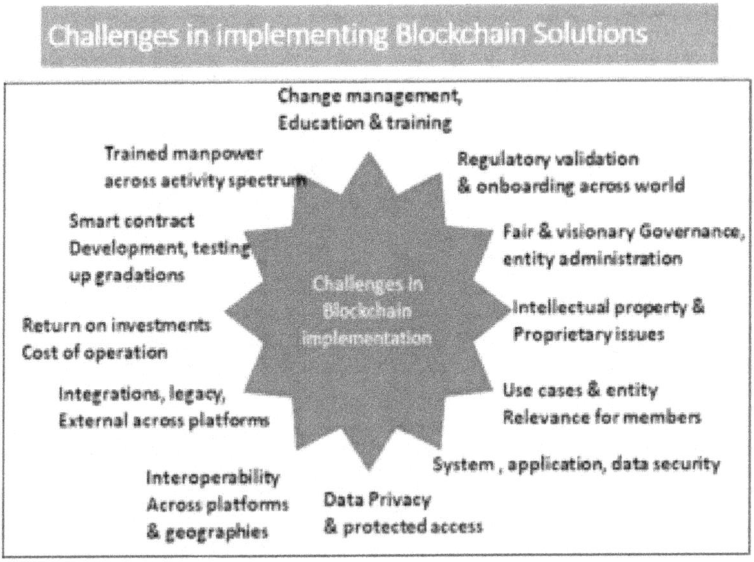

Fig 10.1: Key challenges faced while implementing Blockchain applications

In January 2020, World Economic Forum presented a report that took stock of the developments in Blockchain adoption in UAE.

It has noted that, "Blockchain has swept the UAE as one of the most promising technologies for digital transformation. Government entities, banks, telecommunications providers and academia have begun exploring the applications of blockchain at an unprecedented rate. The results have been staggering, in both the public and private sectors – with more than 40 government entities and 120 blockchain companies covering 200-plus initiatives."

The Centre for the Fourth Industrial Revolution UAE surveyed over 100 stakeholders from more than 60 various governmental and non-governmental entities across the country actively exploring or implementing blockchain. The primary purpose of the survey was to understand the maturity of the ecosystem and the relevant challenges and key success factors at hand.

The following figure provided by the WEF report summarises the key challenges faced while implementing Blockchain based solutions by various stake holders.

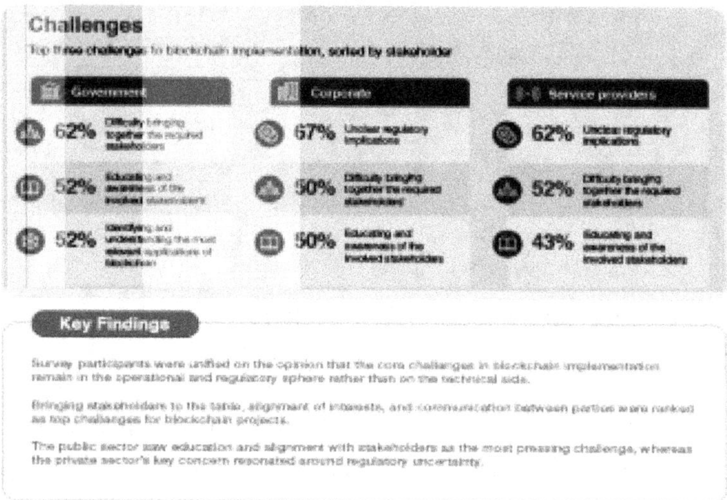

Fig 10.2: Key Challenges faced in Blockchain implementation (Source: WEF report on UAE Jan 2020)

The challenges faced are as per the decreasing order of intensity are summarised in the following figure.

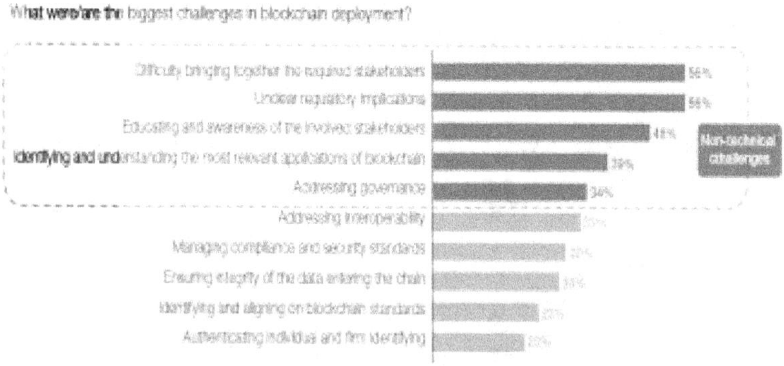

Fig 10.3: Blockchain implementation Challenges

Source: Inclusive Deployment of Blockchain, Case studies and

Learnings from UAE.

Over 52% of the projects surveyed were in the post implementation stage and the following figure identifies the key factors behind the success of the various projects being implemented.

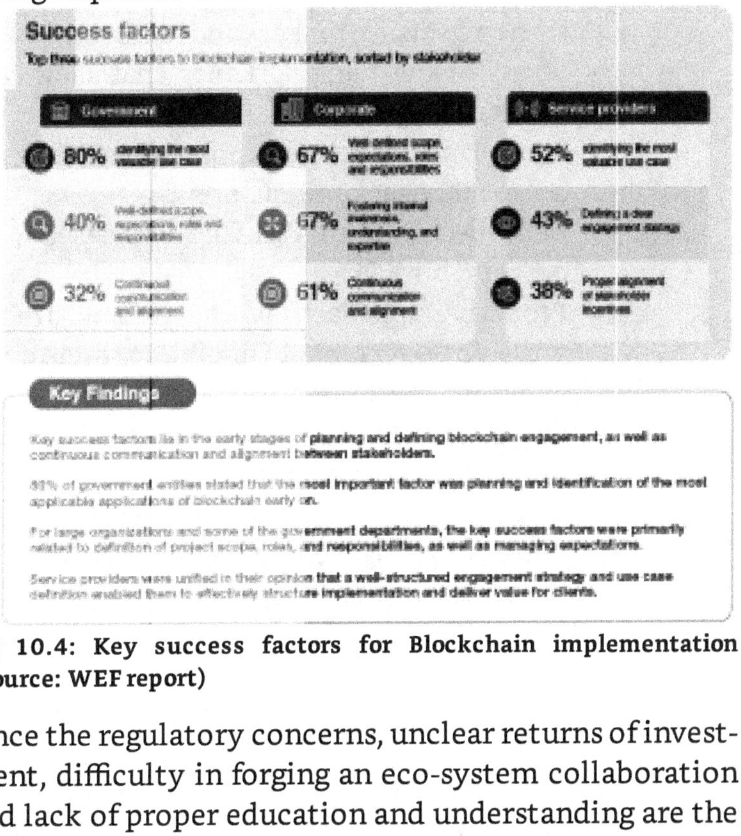

Fig 10.4: Key success factors for Blockchain implementation (Source: WEF report)

Since the regulatory concerns, unclear returns of investment, difficulty in forging an eco-system collaboration and lack of proper education and understanding are the key factors hampering the Blockchain adoption, Governments across the world have to come together and take proactive steps in facilitating and regulating the Blockchain ecosystems. They should actively participate in global initiatives led by United Nations, UNDP, WEF, WHO, UNICEF and such others to foster a climate of co-development and co-evolution that will hasten the accelerated adoption of Blockchain.

- Increasing Exposure to global adoption use cases through government targeted seminars, conferences
- Spreading Blockchain awareness and education to decision makers and facilitators
- Stress of ow hanging fruits that facilitate quicker adoption
- Focus on Blockchain applications that require nil Legacy migrations
- Demonstration of Tangible Use cases with perceptible ROI.
- Proactive approach by engaging with Progressive Government Officials through cost-effective, low obligation Pilots.
- Collaborating with Governments to come out with white papers & practical use case studies
- Increasing engagement with Academia & collaborating to offer cutting edge & high impact but economical solutions to Government
- Subsidizing infrastructure and Proactively collaborating with other Government & Public sector organisations to collaborate with promising Start-ups, venture funds and interested organisations to help develop cost-effective PoCs (Proof of Concepts), Pilots with assured buy-back arrangements.

CHAPTER 11: ENCOURAGING BLOCKCHAIN ADOPTION & EDUCATING THE NEW GENERATION FOR ADOPTION

To develop applications in new generation technologies involves tremendous innovation and encouragement for disruptive application development orientation. Often this involves a lot of investment and involvement of the brightest minds to continuously imagine new possibilities and push the frontiers of technology and research.

Start-ups are best placed to engage in such activities, but they need to be backed by a tremendous push and support from the Government.

Regulatory Sandbox is a platform that is promoted by most of the developed and progressive countries that offers a lot of facilities to the start-ups to quickly develop their validated ideas with an added incentive of government led adoption, if they are proven to have a high chance of success.

A regulatory sandbox is a regulatory approach, typically summarized in writing and published, that allows live, time-bound testing of innovations under a regulator's oversight. Novel financial products, technologies, and business models can be tested under a set of rules, supervision requirements, and appropriate safeguards.

- A sandbox creates a conducive and contained space where incumbents and challengers experiment with innovations at the edge or even outside of the existing regulatory framework.
- A regulatory sandbox brings the cost of innovation down, reduces barriers to entry, and allows regulators

to collect important insights before deciding if further regulatory action is necessary.
• A successful test may result in several outcomes, including full-fledged or tailored authorization of the innovation, changes in regulation, or a cease-and desist order.
(Reference; United Nations Secretary-General's Special Advocate for Inclusive Finance for Development briefing on Regulatory Sandbox).
Let us now examine a case study of how Singapore, one of the leading Digital Nations and ranked the Smartest city in the world consistently by IMD, implements a Sandbox to encourage innovators to develop and launch disruptive technology-based products.
Ranked #1 in the world for ease of doing business, Singapore has many incentives for budding entrepreneurs that allows the innovation to be commercialised in a speedy manner.
All the entrepreneurs are well encouraged to propose their new ideas to a seasoned set of Public-Private mentor networks and the selected ideas are put through a well-designed Sand Box system with
immense Government support, to examine viability & potential of the envisaged solutions. Once the ideas are proven in the Sandbox, they are immediately primed for implementation with the full force of Government behind them as a facilitator, adopter, funder, and implementer.

How does the Regulatory Sandbox Work?
Case study: Regulatory Sandbox – EMA (Energy Metering Authority, Govt of Singapore)
(https://www.ema.gov.sg/media_release.aspx?news_sid=20171020Wab84AqS9NXY)

1. Regulatory Sandbox enables the energy sector to test new products & services in the electricity & gas sectors, before deciding on the appropriate regulatory treatment.
2. This is designed to help the innovators to leverage on new technology or apply existing technology in novel ways to create value for electricity and gas consumers, or to improve business and operational procedures, without the risk of a major failure that normally stifle such innovations
3. EMA is encouraging innovators to apply for such experimentation by enabling such ideas to be tested through a Regulatory Sandbox. A successful application would allow the idea to be applied in the market, while being subject to relaxed regulatory requirements, in a controlled environment that limits the risks to consumers and industry.
4. The evaluation criteria for ideas applying for the Regulatory Sandbox include whether the proposal:
i. Uses technologies/products in an innovative way.
ii. Addresses a problem or brings benefits to consumers and/or the energy sector.
iii. Requires some changes to existing rules; and
iv. Has assessed and mitigated foreseeable risks.

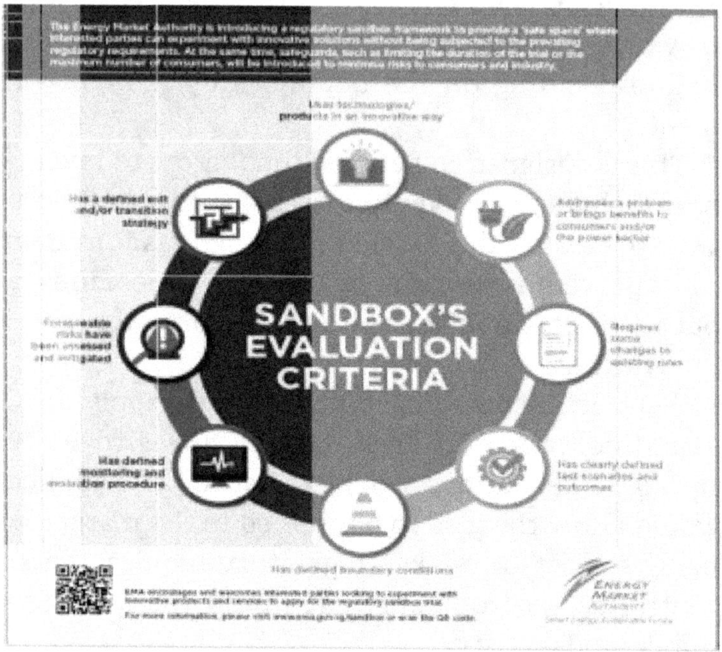

Fig 11.1 EMA Regulatory Sandbox

5. The Regulatory Sandbox will help EMA adjust its regulatory frameworks to keep pace with advances in technology and enable promising innovations to prosper.

6. The Regulatory Sandbox will complement ongoing Energy Research and Development (R&D) initiatives, by providing a platform for R&D projects to be tested on a broader scale in Singapore. This system attracts the best organisations, entrepreneurs and investors in the World that further fuels the innovation with high quality and chance of success. With focus on the ABCD of today's disruptive technologies namely API economy, Blockchain, Cloud & Data Analytics enveloped in a highly guarded Cyber security focused approach, Singapore leads in the adoption of these technologies towards a better quality of life for its citizens and the global population!

Today Singapore continues to thrive, guided by the values of openness, inclusiveness, self-determination, meritocracy, and incorruptibility.

Educating the Nation- Government's role

The Role of Academic Institutions in Achieving the Targets for Advanced Technologies:

India has a very good academic structure when it comes to AI but the outcome in terms of innovation and Intellectual Property (IP) is on a lower side. India is not focusing on creating IPs or Advanced Technology products at the academic level. A centre for excellence in this sector will be very helpful but it should be thoroughly monitored by government.

IISc, IIT Mumbai, IIT Kanpur, IIT Patna, IIT Delhi, IIT Madras, some IIITs and a few central universities are leading the efforts of the academia in India. However, the number of research papers and patentable solutions developed in the Indian academic ecosystem is considered miniscule compared to the leading countries in the world

like US, China and the D5 nations. The research conducted by the Indian academic institutions is hampered by the siloed approach and the lack of coordination between the Industry, academia, and Start-up ecosystem & is disjointed from the real-life situations where the difference can be perceptible. The number of solutions developed through the research in India; that has been commercialized on large scale to generate value; is dismal. This also leads to the reluctance of the industry and government to engage with substantial investments that can produce cognizable results. There should be a clear value proposition for the enterprises to partner with the Academia for coinvesting in developing disruptive technology solutions.

Role of Blockchain in Digital Transformation:
Distributed Ledger technologies like Blockchain enable risk management by offering controlled access, fool proof authentication and trusted authorization for those involved and transactions conducted between them by acting as a trusted third party. Digital transformation at scale can thus be expedited in a secured manner. The following are some of the crucial activities to be done by Government of India to support path breaking applications of Distributed Ledger Technologies:

●● Unique Blockchain based self-sovereign digital identities for all citizens

●● Central bank digital currency on a national permissioned Blockchain

●● Regulatory recognition of data and transaction records stored on Blockchain.

This will help in eliminating corruption & inefficiency linked leakages, thus, unlocking huge government resources that may be otherwise wasted or are spent unproductively. Blockchain enables availability of high-quality data for AI and ML applications. Trust and transparency offered by Blockchain, as well as secured private digital identities (of devices and people) offers high quality record keeping, an integral component for several applications in Financial, Supply chain and in Health care applications like clinical record management, and electronic health records administration.

Reinventing Careers through Re-Skilling:
Realising that change is the only constant in today's fast evolving world, knowledge professionals should upskill

themselves to stay relevant in a world. Some of the activities that are suggested are outlined below:

1. Keep abreast of the latest use cases by studying the way the global leaders like Amazon, Netflix, Facebook, Google, JPMorgan, HSBC etc., are leveraging emerging technologies.
2. Keep abreast of the tools and platforms offered by leading companies in the field like IBM, Google, Microsoft, Intel etc.
3. Undertake courses on Online platforms to upskill on the trending topics in the emerging technologies.
4. Study how AI/ML & Blockchain applications are being implemented in leading countries like China, USA, Singapore & Middle East.
5. Always look proactively for opportunities to implement AI/ML solutions in practical scenarios while being sensitive to the way, various businesses are leveraging the same.
6. Learn to be computer literate and try to pick up a language like Node JS, Golang or Python.
7. Try to write articles, white papers or books that will force one to conduct intense research around related topics.

Role of Government in Encouraging Skilling, Reskilling and Upskilling

There is a large need to take care of the existing workforce that is likely to be displaced from their jobs due to the emerging technology led automation. Professionals have a dire need to re-skill & stay relevant. Hence it is imperative for the Government to put in place a concerted strategy to deliver appropriate competence & impart he industry relevant skill while encouraging the learners to master the same. It is imperative to partner Global leading educational/training providers and offer the highest quality programs that combine theoretical, practical, and cutting-edge solutioning capabilities to the executives across the various stages of the corporate lifecycle.

1. Reskilling should be encouraged through proper incentives and opportunity for career growth
2. Formal and informal education with highest standards should be made available with proper standardization and recognized certification that is valued by industry.
3. Online education through MOOCs should be blended with real life opportunities to explore and implement solutions on job.

In conclusion, while it is true that COVID-19 pandemic has resulted in a dramatic paradigm shift in the form of increased digitalisation & automation, times have also become very challenging due to the
availability of multiple resources across the software development lifecycle with the proliferation of open-source technologies and highly secure and scalable cloud enabled SAAS environment.

While countries like India have understood the paradigm of Smart Cities and Digital Governance, they have a long way to go as far as implementation is concerned, It is here that the examples set
by countries like Estonia, Dubai (UAE), Singapore (which is also the Smartest city in the world) must closely studied, understood and evaluated for implementation. Sustainable Development is very much required if the world must survive into the future and we manage to handover a safe and secure world to our younger generations.

Hence, we need to consciously strive to achieve Sustainable development like the way Singapore is planning 50 years in advance and is overcoming a number of geographic limitations as well as resource constraints. It is indeed possible to overturn the tide of environmental degradation caused by industrial development and this has been stressed in every chapter in this book through real life examples that are in vogue.

CONCLUSION

Distributed Ledger technologies like Blockchain enable risk management by offering controlled access, fool proof authentication and trusted authorization for those involved and facilitate secured transactions between them by acting as a trusted third party. Digital transformation at scale can thus be expedited in a secured manner.

The following are some of the crucial activities to be done by Governments to support path breaking applications of Distributed Ledger Technologies:

- Unique Blockchain based self-sovereign digital identities for all citizens
- Central bank digital currency on a national permissioned Blockchain
- Regulatory recognition of data and transaction records stored on Blockchain .

This will help is eliminating corruption & inefficiency linked leakages, thus unlocking huge government resources that may be otherwise wasted or are spent unproductively.

Blockchain enables availability of high-quality data for AI and ML applications. Trust and transparency offered by Blockchain, as well as secured private digital identities (of devices and people) offers high quality record keeping, an integral component for several applications in Financial, Supply chain and in Health care applications like clinical record management, and electronic health records administration.

In this book we have examined the process of implementing Blockchain application using Design thinking methodology and also got an idea about the Blockchain applications being implemented in several leading countries.

Blockchain adoption is still in the nascent stage and there can be an exhaustive resource to learn about it in a comprehensive manner . It keeping evolving continuously and several new developments are underway. Hence, we need to have a mindset of continuous experimentation, openness to learn and a tolerance to ambiguity that allows us to adapt and stay in tune with the technological advancements. The core objective should be to leverage the best available technologies for the welfare of our citizens.

It is heartening to note the developments in implementing Blockchain across multiple eGovernance use cases in benefiting the citizens as well as businesses.

China, UAE (Dubai emirates), Estonia, Singapore & Thailand stand out in this regard and the rest of the countries can leverage on the experience of their learnings.

ANNEXURE 1: MODEL BLOCKCHAIN COUNTRY- CASE STUDY OF THAILAND

No discussion on Blockchain across Governments is complete without closely examining the rapid strides Thailand is making to explore , extract and experience the Power of Blockchain in all its glory.

I am extremely thankful to my close friend and ex-teammate, Sanat Bhat, a key member of IBM Thailand's Blockchain Solutioning team, who has helped me in unravelling the immense potential of Blockchain through the actions being undertaken by Thailand's Government and progressive Financial system.

Thailand is indeed setting an example to the whole world about how to facilitate and manage the Blockchain

Thailand government is seeking to unlock the nation's economic potential, by leveraging the power of blockchain technology for the implementation of Thailand 4.0.

In keeping with Thailand 4.0's emphasis on the use of digital technologies to spur national economic growth and development, blockchain has a critical role to play as catalysts for the promotion of digital innovation in Thailand. Leading by example, the Thai government is experimenting with using distributed ledgers in the operations of its various state agencies.

In August 2017, Thailand Post, the country's state enterprise for postal services, introduced the use of blockchain for its warehousing, sorting, shipping, and delivery processes with the aim of enhancing operational efficiency. Another notable government initiative had the

Electronic Transactions Development Agency (ETDA) sign a Memorandum of Understanding (MoU) with local blockchain start-up Omise Co., Ltd. to build a national electronic Know-Your-Customer (e-KYC) platform, as part of the ETDA's Digital ID project.

Other than state agencies, blockchain use has also been taking place at the ministerial level. In October last year, the Ministry of Commerce announced that it is exploring the feasibility of using blockchain in the areas of copyright, agriculture, and trade finance to boost the country's credibility in terms of intellectual property as well as the overall competitiveness of Thai businesses. Around the same time, the Ministry of Finance announced that it is planning to use blockchain to track tax payments for the purpose of detecting tax fraud.

Fast forward to January 2020, the Ministry of Science and Technology's National Electronics and Computer Technology Center (NECTEC) announced that it has developed a blockchain-based voting system. It has been looking for trial partners to test out the system on a smaller scale, such as in elections for universities, provinces, local communities, etc.

Aside from public administration, the Bank of Thailand (BoT), which is the country's central bank, is also spearheading the use of blockchain for Thailand's banking and finance industry. The BoT has been collaborating with eight local banks through an undertaking dubbed "Project Inthanon." The project was launched in August 2018 with the objective of exploring the use of blockchain's Proof of Concept (PoC) framework to develop a Central Bank Digital Currency (CBDC) for domestic wholesale fund transfers.

Phase I of Project Inthanon, which was completed

in January 2020, involved the development of a CBDC prototype using R3's Corda blockchain platform. The results of the tests showed that the use of blockchain has the potential to enhance the efficiency of interbank payment transfers, particularly during off-hours.

Phase II, which started in February this year and is expected to be completed by September, involves exploring the use of blockchain-based debt instruments issued by the BoT to reduce delivery and settlement times for interbank trading and repurchase transactions. Additionally, Phase II studies the use of blockchain for regulatory compliance and data reconciliation, particularly to facilitate the reconciliation by banks of its customer accounts with its money transfer records as part of its compliance obligations under BoT regulations.

The final phase, i.e. Phase III, commenced in August this year and is expected to be completed by the end of this year. This phase entails a collaboration between the BoT and the Hong Kong Monetary Authority (HKMA) to explore the use of blockchain for the development of interoperable ledgers for cross-border fund transfers.

With 10% of Thais owning cryptocurrencies in one form or another, it is clear that the technology will have a role to play in shaping the Thai way of life. Given the advances made by the government and central bank in embracing the potential of blockchain, it may be just a matter of time before the Southeast Asian country escapes its various traps and propel its economy towards its Thailand 4.0 ambitions.

1.BODIES TO REGULATE BLOCKCHAIN PROJECTS IN THAILAND

Thailand has 3 Blockchain bodies that regulate the projects for Ministry of Finance.

A. Blockchain Community Initiative

3 years back several banks created the Thailand Blockchain Community Initiative(BCI). This week The Nation reported that 22 banks are now involved including foreign bank branches. BCI was responsible to approve all nation scale Blockchain projects for financial services in Thailand.

The first application was for Letters of Guarantee (LG). The aim was to halve the costs involved in using the trade finance tool. Other benefits include reducing fraud and speeding up the process of issuing LGs.

Every year in Thailand, there are more than 500,000 LGs issued worth more than Baht 1.3 trillion ($43.2 billion). The aim is to digitize 50% of these within three years. The group is chaired by Predee Daochai who chairman of the Thai Bankers' Association is also. So far, testing was executed as part of the Bank of Thailand's sandbox and is expected to go into production within the sandbox in June.

To ensure a broad range of stakeholders, the project involves several state enterprises and large corporates including from the electricity, oil and chemical sectors. Accenture and IBM Thailand helped with the project, which is based on Hyperledger Fabric.

The consortium has now incorporated with six shareholder banks, Bangkok Bank, Krungthai, Bank of

Ayudhya, Kasikornbank, TMB and Siam Commercial.

Several of these banks are involved in other blockchain initiatives. Bangkok Bank is part of both the Marco Polo and Voltrontrade finance consortia. State-owned Krungthaihas a cross border payments project. And Siam Commercialis working with Accenture on a procurement blockchain.

Sixteen additional banks will use the platform. They are Kiatnakin Bank, Citibank, CIMB Thai, Sumitomo Mitsui Banking Corp, Tisco, Thanachart, BNP Paribas, Bank for Agriculture and Agricultural Cooperatives, Export-Import Bank of Thailand, Mizuho Bank, United Overseas Bank (Thai), Land and Houses Bank, Standard Chartered (Thai), Government Savings Bank, Industrial and Commercial Bank of China (Thai) and HSBC.

The milestones of setting up the BCI were:

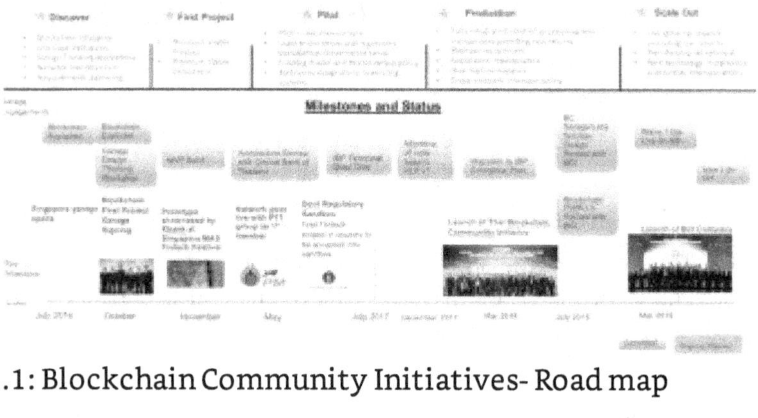

1.1: Blockchain Community Initiatives- Road map

B. ETDA

Electronic Transaction Development Agency (ETDA) is a nodal entity set up under the Electronic Transaction Act for regulating the electronic transaction in the country.

ETDA is supposed to start implement Self Sovereign Identity based Digital Corporate ID network for the country. http://thailaws.com/law/t_laws/tlaw16079.pdf

C. ITMX

National ITMX Company Limited (NITMX) was originally founded under the name ATM Pool Company Limited in 1993. Subsequently, in July 2005, the company was renamed National ITMX Company Limited to expand and extend the scope of the company's business and products. Specifically, NITMX was created to satisfy Thailand's requirement to keep up with continuing global advancement in electronic commerce and payment systems. The shareholders of National ITMX are local commercial banks in Thailand.

Under direction from the Bank of Thailand, National ITMX is set up to be the key infrastructure and central data processing system that exchanges, manages, and processes data across Member Banks /organizations in order to support various interbank services.

NITMX is working with Thai Bankers Association (TBA) and member banks to establish "National Digital Trade Platform" (focusing on bank related business) to improve banks operations services and support new business.

The Company offers the following products and services to its member banks:

- Single Payment System Services
- Bulk Payment System Services
- Local Switching System Services
- NSW Bank Gateway System Services
- Card Fraud Monitoring and Detection Services

- ITMX e-GP Bank Gateway
- PromptPay
- PromptCard

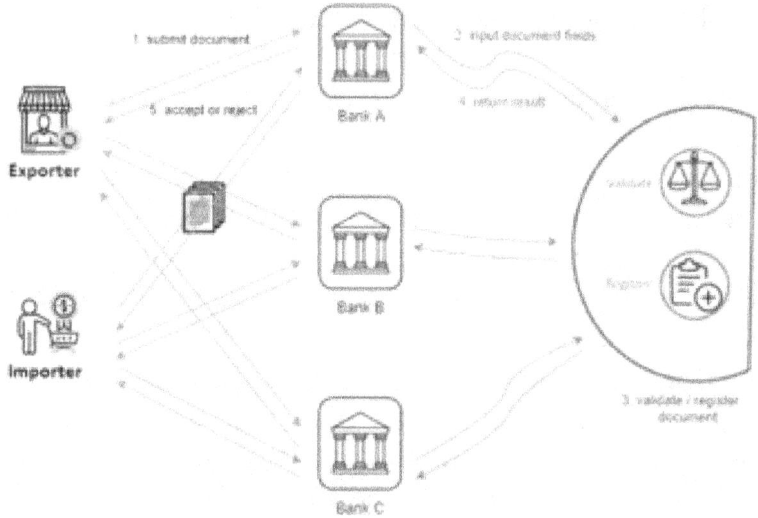

1.2: NDTP Blockchain Project by NDMX
for Cross Border Trade facilitation

The NDTP for banking will be established to improve cross-border trade financing process and fraud prevention for banks. The conceptual flow explains a standard process and relevant actors of NDTP, more information following details.

1. Exporters / Importers submit financing requests and supporting documents to banks.
2. Banks input the supporting document fields whether they have been financed before via platform's API or web portal or Blockchain node.
3. The platform validates each submitted

document by querying and comparing against the registered documents.

4. The platform will return duplicate status when an identical document is found (based on the defined business logic for document comparison for each document type). The platform will return the new document status when cannot find any similar document.
5. Banks then make the decision for financing requests based on the provided information from the platform.

Parts for the project:

<u>Transaction Flow for Document Registration, Validation & Cancellation are depicted as follows:</u>

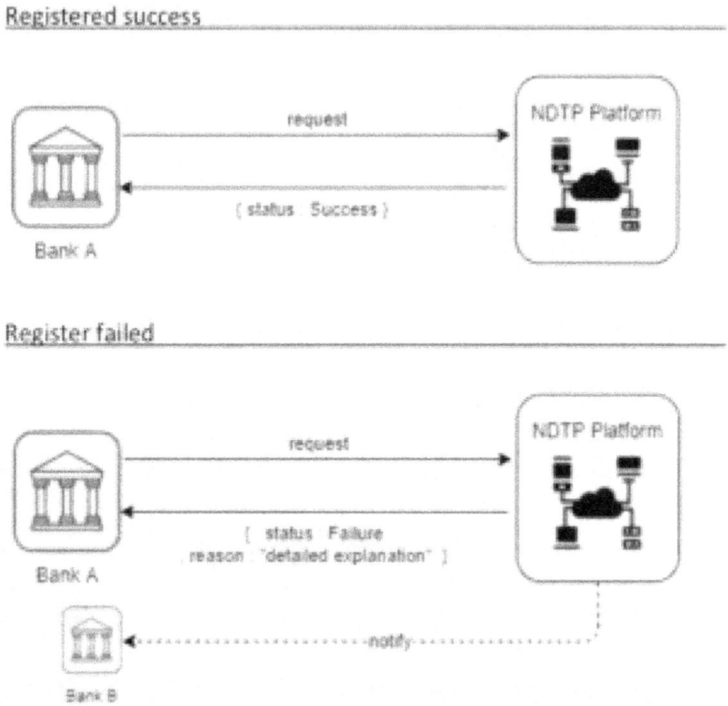

1.3: Document Registration over Blockchain

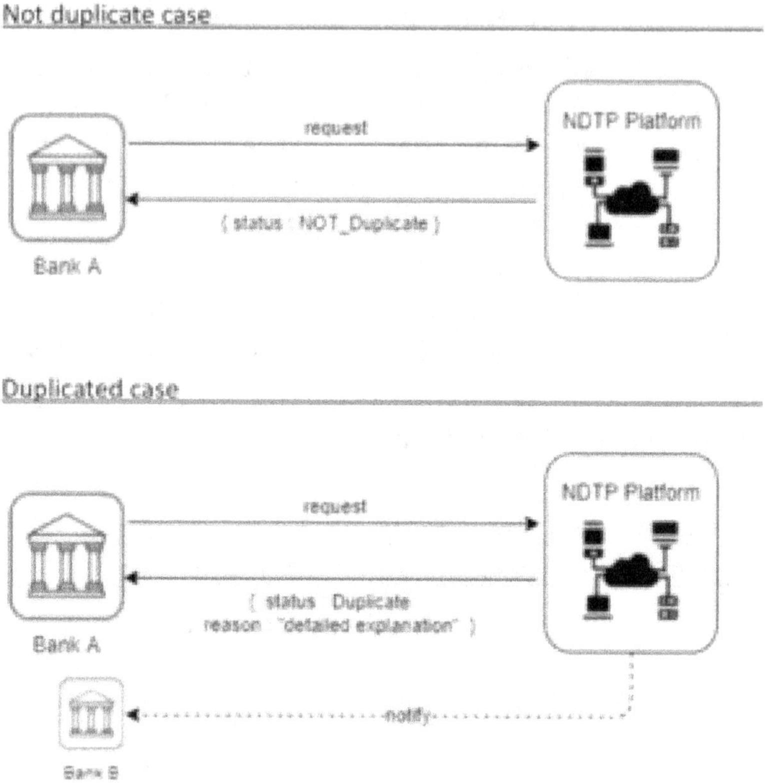

1.4: Document Validation over Blockchain

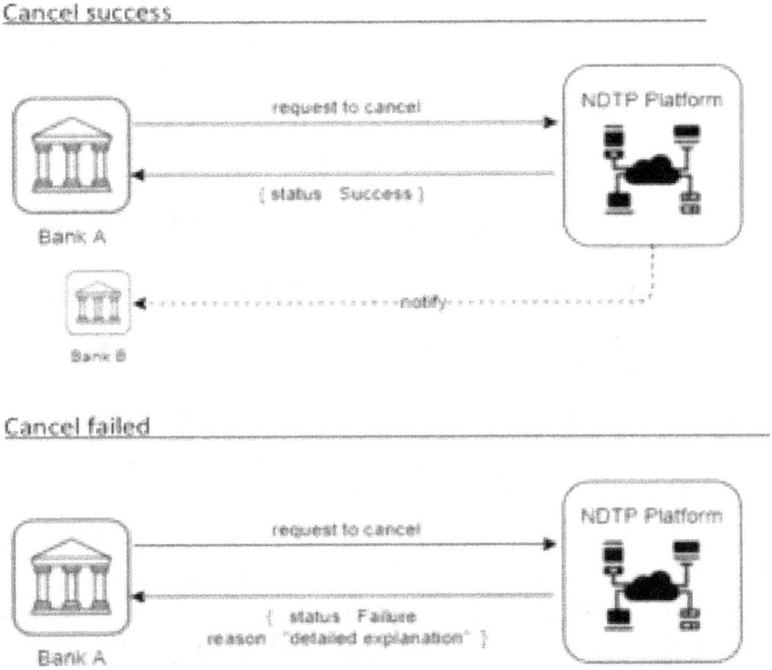

1.5: Document Cancellation over Blockchain

2. NATION SCALE BLOCKCHAIN PROJECTS IMPLEMENTED

A) Savings Bond Platform for the country

As part of the mission to prepare its people for disruptive technologies, Bank of Thailand (BOT) has started to look at the benefits of distributed ledger technology (DLT) and blockchain technology.

BOT expects blockchain technology to enable all stakeholders to have access to the same information, increasing efficiency and transparency.

BOT has selected the savings bond sales processes as its first use case. Bonds-related processes are complex, with many parties participating in the ecosystem, including selling agents, BOT and the Thailand Securities Depository, amongst others.

It now takes 15 days for investors to receive their bonds after receiving allocation.

Once completed, this initiative will help increase efficiency, whilst also reducing the total operating costs of the entire system, and it will be developed later on to form the basis for Thailand's market infrastructure for government and corporate securities. This is one of the world's first uses of blockchain technology in the field of government savings bond sales.

BOT has collaborated with related organizations, including the Public Debt Management Office (PDMO), Thailand Securities Depository (TSD) and selling agents. This was accomplished by BOT and IBM contributing to the development of this system using blockchain, and facilitated through Design Thinking methodology, enabling teams to understand the challenges and requirements of all stakeholders.

The DLT Scripless Bond project benefits all stakeholders. Investors will be able to receive their bonds faster – it takes 15 days now and will be only 2 days in the future. They will also be purchase bonds up to their full allocation rights from any bank. Selling agents, TSD and BOT will also be able to reduce processing time and workloads. Bond issuers will also be able to manage bond issues faster and stimulate increased competition between selling agents. Overall, the system will lead to reduced operating costs across the entire value chain with greater security.

This important milestone leads to the digital economy and society. Based on these key benefits, blockchain technology can successfully move the settlement cycle of government savings bonds from trade date plus 15 days (T+15) toward T+2 with improved management, security, and privacy. This is the first and important step in a journey of discovery.

BOT analyzed many use cases and observed that the Thai government savings bond sales process had several points of friction that blockchain could potentially resolve. It is a time-consuming process that relies on a non-real-time system, has duplicate validation steps, with manual reconciliation requirements prone to data errors. Delivery of savings bonds to investors currently takes 15 days, whilst other government bonds issues can be delivered in just two days according to market best practice.

Consequently, in early 2018, BOT initiated the DLT Scripless Bond Project and conducted a proof of concept around blockchain technology. The project was built with Hyperledger Fabric, an open-source blockchain framework implementation, as the foundation of its prototype to assess potential benefits and business values which could potentially improve operational efficiency. The project was driven by BOT and supported by key industry participants employing their considerable expertise and experience. Key stakeholders and their roles/responsibilities in this project are:

1. Bank of Thailand (BOT): registrar and paying agent
2. Thailand Securities Depository (TSD): Central Securities Depository (CSD) and ISIN/CFI code registration
3. Public Debt Management Office (PDMO): bond issuer
4. Bangkok Bank (BBL), Kasikorn Bank (KBank), Krungthai Bank (KTB) and Siam Commercial Bank (SCB): selling agents
5. Thai Bond Market Association (ThaiBMA): bond symbol registration
6. IBM: technology partner
7. Leveraging the significant experience of IBM in enterprise blockchain solutions, this collaborative project employed IBM as a technical partner jointly managing the project and co-designing and developing solutions with BOT.

A.1. Objectives

1. The DLT Scripless Bond Project aimed not only to enable BOT to gain deeper insights and develop capabilities and

the implications of using blockchain technologies, as well as potential benefits in reducing overall costs to the industry, as well as maximizing operational process efficiencies.

2. In order to identify both weaknesses and opportunities for blockchain technology, the project prototype was designed and developed with the following key features:
3. Data integration and bookkeeping: to integrate all relevant data as the single source of truth and record all transaction activities
4. Real-time information accessibility: to access information in near real-time to enable more rapid analysis and more effective management
5. Smart contracts & automation: to facilitate more effective operations through smart contracts so as to maximise reduction of manual intervention.
6. Reports and monitoring: to monitor information and enable visibility to authorized participants (on a 'need-to-know' basis).
7. If there is sufficient technical and business value, replacement of the existing government savings bond sales operations with a blockchain solution might be considered and scaled out to

other types of government bond services in the future.

A.2 Approach

Design Thinking was one of the methodologies used in the DLT Scripless Bond project to gain an empathic understanding of pains and problems in all aspects. All key stakeholders were engaged to provide their experiences and motivations.

After brainstorming and discussion, the issues of redundant validation, data quality, data exchange, and reconciliation in the processing of government savings bond sales were uncovered. Major aspects were identified and targeted for improvement of operational processes and investor satisfaction: speed of sales transactions, data quality, and transparency of bond sales information.

After collection of these requirements, a new set of processes (future state) was developed for government savings bond sales, forming the basis for the prototype development.

Another methodology used was agile development. The prototype was developed in multiple scaled-down iterations with specific features which were evolved over time. The development team had to complete each iteration and made it ready for review periodically so that the prototype could be adapted, using feedback and updated requirements of key stakeholders. Developing the prototype with agile development allowed investigation of the solution, identified any potential weaknesses, and updated solution before the completed prototype was delivered.

A.3 Functional scope

The proof of concept was focused on two key processes: bond registration and bond sales. Bond registration required digitization of paper documents including bond profiles and selling criteria according to prospectus applied to savings bonds. Once these data had been set up and finalized, they became the basis for a single source of truth for network participants to proceed to the next steps of the bond sales process.

Bond sales had four sequential processes: bond sales and reservation, securities account opening, payments, and bond depository.

During the sales process, shared information about specific bonds, such as issuance and remaining amount of sales could be accessed in real time. All sales transactions would

be validated in smart contracts before being committed to the network. Bonds could be reserved on a first-come, first-served basis.

The process of securities account opening was conducted automatically with smart contracts. Processing of payment and bond depository were handled externally by existing systems and Application Programming Interfaces (APIs) were developed to integrate them with the blockchain network.

A management dashboard was provided to all stakeholders for access on a need-to-know basis to all relevant information and transactional status at every step of the bond registration and bond sales processes.

A.4 Process design

Handling multiple and concurrent reservation orders is a non-trivial requirement and presented opportunities for innovative approaches from a technology and business process engineering perspective.

To ensure the reservation order system for government savings bonds is sufficiently robust, secure, and efficient for all, it was investigated to see whether or not adjustments to the remaining amount and allocations to individual investors was properly captured.

Business requirements were formulated through Design Thinking exercises with key stakeholders. Ongoing engagement, including feedback and detailed discussion, developed a more comprehensive understanding of stakeholder issues, concerns, and expectations relating to the new processes and potential solution. Using this working model, all key stakeholders agreed to reduce the savings bond settlement cycle from trade date plus 15 days (T+15) to T+2, in line with international market best practice.

After the Design Thinking workshop and subsequent participant feedback, the main features considered to be opportunities for improving process efficiency and transparency were as follows:

- Single validation: this feature allowed participants to validate any transaction by using the same validation requirements set in the smart contracts before a transaction was committed to a ledger. No more additional application for validation was required.
- Single source of information: all participants would be able to access the same information, such as bond profiles, selling criteria, and remaining amount. The information was updated near real time and provided improved transparency for management.
- Common standard within the blockchain network: one set of standards was adopted for data format, reference data, and transactional data used in business processes to improve data quality and remove inefficiencies from digital business.

- Flexible information management: before the process of bond depository, all sales transactions were editable to allow flexibility in timing of processing. Selling agents could update details as required. Any time a modification was made, the sales transaction would be digitally time-stamped and recorded for transaction transparency.

Finally, T+2 processes and all operational improvements relating to bond registration and bond sales were designed according to the key elements and considerations illustrated below:

a. **Bond registration**

Prior to the sales of any government savings bond, the issuer is required to provide full disclosure of the bond profile and selling criteria that will be automatically created as smart contracts. Next, ThaiBMA will assign a unique bond symbol. After the bond symbol is assigned, the registrar requests the International Securities Identification Number (ISIN) and Classification of Financial Instruments (CFI codes) from a CSD. Finally, at the end of the bond registration process, the issuer will officially approve the publication of the relevant information for every stakeholder to use.

b. **Bond sales (T to T+2)**

Sales and reservations (T)

During the sales period, all relevant information for sales, remaining amount, and purchasing quota for each individual investor is retrievable in real time. To reserve a bond allocation, selling agents are required to check whether there is sufficient quantity available for each purchase order, and that the order does not exceed the investor individual purchasing quota.

Once a transaction is processed into the blockchain network, it will be validated against the selling criteria set in the smart contracts, to ensure that investors are eligible for allocation according to the prospectus. If all conditions and criteria are satisfied, the bonds will be reserved on a first-come, first-served basis and the remaining amount (starts with the issuance amount of bonds) will be immediately offset by the amount purchased. Once committed to the sales transaction ledger, transactions are visible to the registrar and CSD for any further action.

Securities account opening (T to T+1)

In the case of new investors, selling agents are required to provide specific details to open a securities account - this can be completed whilst making a bond reservation or on the next day (T+1) but must be done prior to the depository to enable flexibility for selling agents. Once the information has been confirmed by selling agents, CSD will be notified by smart contracts to open securities accounts in real time and in turn notify the status back to selling agents and registrar.

Payments (T)

At close of business, the total allocated amount of bonds and funds will be reconciled to the subscribed orders.

All selling agents will then be notified and required to make payment to the registrar. The registrar will then transfer

the funds received to the issuer. In this proof of concept, the funds transfer was performed externally. The payment status would then be returned to the blockchain network for next steps.

Bond depository (T+1) and delivery (T+2)

On T+1, CSD will be notified at a fixed time to credit bonds into investors' securities accounts and then notify selling agents of the transaction status. As certain action is required away from the blockchain network after bonds are successfully credited into securities accounts, investors will be able to update their balances with their selling agents on the *next business day (T+2).*

A. 4 Design considerations

Within the focused areas of this project, bond registration and bond sales, the solution was designed to consider the value of blockchain capabilities in the following technical domains:

- Accessing information on the blockchain network
- Prevention of duplicate reservations of bond sales and exceeding quota
- High throughput for bond sales and reservations
- Data privacy and cross-channel communication
- Message notification on blockchain

A.5. Technical observations and key findings

Accessing information on the blockchain network

Hyperledger Fabric offers Software Development Kits (SDKs) in various programming languages such as Node.js or Java to interact with a blockchain network.

Prevention of duplicate reservations of bond sales and exceeding quota:

One of the most important factors in designing the blockchain prototype of government savings bond sales was to ensure data integrity and to prevent duplications, which could occur if an attempt were made to reserve the same asset in the ledger. The other consideration was to ensure that bonds sales and reservations did not exceed the available quota for bond sales. Concerning bond sales and reservations, each selling agent was required to verify that the remaining amount was sufficient to accept each individual for reservations across different sales channels. Once a selling agent submitted a sales transaction to the blockchain network, the remaining amount would be offset by the reserved amount and this deducted amount would be used as an initial number in calculation for the next transaction. Thus, the remaining amount must be accurate even when many concurrent transactions were submitted simultaneously by selling agents.

In the assessment, a new bond issue was created with an issue size of 100,000 baht. To simulate five selling agents making reservations, five concurrent transactions with reserved amounts of 1,000 baht each were submitted to the blockchain network within one second of each other. The transactions were allowed to complete and the subsequent test iterations were started after a one second pause. Ten iterations were done and assessed.

The assessment revealed that 15 transactions were committed to the ledger and when checking the remaining amount, the new value of 85,000 baht was recorded.

This meant that the solution prototype worked correctly by deducting the accurate number of 15,000 (15 x 1,000) baht from 100,000 baht.

A read-write set is generated once an endorser executes the transaction. The read set contains a list of unique keys together with their committed versions of data whilst

the write set contains a list of unique keys and their new values written in the transaction. Transactions are verified upon commit to ensure that the data that has been read is still valid and has not been modified by other transactions since. Due to the read-write set semantics, this assessment showed that transactions submitted at the same time all contain in their read sets the same unique key and a committed version of remaining amount asset. Once one of the concurrent transactions was committed to the ledger, the version of its unique key would be changed to a new one. For this reason, the other transactions with the read set containing the previous version of unique key would be marked as invalid, changes were not applied to the ledger and the client application would be alerted to retry the transactions if appropriate.

High throughput transactions of bond sales and reservations

During a high demand period, many sales transactions are likely to be submitted through all sales channels of selling agents at the same time. However, due to the limits placed on the amount of bonds issued, bonds will be allocated on a first-come, first-served basis until any new request exceeds the available balance.

In the initial design, two assets were created:

- "RemainingAmount" - for capturing the outstanding balance of bond issuance
- "TransactionDetail" - for recording details of each transaction such as investor name, reserved amount and bond series. Whenever a sales transaction was submitted by a selling agent, an asset

of "TransactionDetail" would be created (add action). Next, the outstanding balance was checked to ensure that the sale was within limits of bond issued (read action). Then the value of "RemainingAmount" asset would be deducted (update action) by the reserved amount and committed the change to a blockchain network.

During peak load, where multiple bond sales requests were submitted by multiple selling agents at the same time, it was observed that the initial design rejected a number of transactions submitted within a short time frame due to the concurrency control mechanism used in Hyperledger Fabric to prevent double-spending. The transactions which were submitted simultaneously would have had the same value of key and version of the "RemainingAmount" asset. If one of them was committed ahead of the others and the value of the version of the "RemainingAmount" asset was changed to the new version, the remaining transactions would be rejected as the transactions tried to update the outdated version. In order to find the most appropriate solution for solving this issue, three more alternatives were designed and assessed as follows:

Alternative solution #1: checking outstanding balance

This approach modified the way that checks were performed to prevent selling more than the available supply of bonds.

Instead of maintaining a running count of the exact balance of unallocated bonds, the total reserved amount was recalculated based on all committed transactions whenever a new transaction was submitted. The reserved balance was then reconciled against the initial issue amount to confirm that there were unsold bonds.

This approach worked for a single transaction, but just like the initial design, it was unable to handle multiple transactions submitted concurrently.

For example, assume a scenario where the total issue size was 20,000,000 baht. Five prior sale transactions with reserved amounts of 1,000,000 baht each have been committed. Subsequently, three new bond reservation transactions of 1,000,000 baht each were submitted concurrently.

For each of the new transactions, the aggregated value of committed transactions (5,000,000 baht) was compared against the bond issue size of 20,000,000 baht to ensure that there were enough unsold bonds.

The result of the outstanding balance calculation was the same for all the three new transactions prior to

the commitment of any of them. However, once any one of these new transactions was successfully committed, the allocated amount would be updated and the two remaining transactions must be rejected as the version number they wish to update was no longer the most current.

Alternative solution #2: par value allocation

This approach stored the number of outstanding bonds instead of the outstanding issue size. For example, for an issue size of 10,000,000 baht, the number of bonds to be sold was 10,000 at a par value of 1,000 baht each.

Therefore, a sale transaction for 50,000 baht would allocate 50 units of the 10,000 bonds outstanding. These 50 units would be individually marked out for the buyer using a random selection process to minimize the probability of a conflict in the allocation process if concurrency was to be supported. Those marked units would not be available for any further transactions.

Several issues were discovered with this approach. First, it took longer to complete a transaction than the other designs. Second, due to the random selection process, there remained a non-zero probability that the same units were marked for different sale transactions submitted concurrently. This would still cause a failure when committing transactions just as in the earlier solution prototypes.

Alternative solution #3: delta commits

To avoid the problem when transactions were submitted concurrently, the booking and confirmation steps was performed into two discrete steps. The solution was designed to use the delta commits approach by committing each transaction without pre-checking the balance retained in the "RemainingAmount" asset.

Incoming transactions were created and queued up with a request status for reservations. Every five seconds, there was an off-chain application running outside the blockchain network to call the specific function used for collecting transactions which were committed during that time. The total amount of bonds required for reservations was then calculated from the committed transactions and checked to see if the remaining amount was sufficient for those reservations to be confirmed. If bonds were still available, each committed transaction would be approved and the remaining amount would be deducted by the reserved amount of the transaction sequentially.

Although this solution prototype could handle the conflict found in the other designs, new issues were identified and needed to be considered. The remaining amount was not updated in real time because the precise figure would be

confirmed after a transaction was committed, so there was a time lag between submission of a transaction and committing it to the blockchain network.

In this case, the selling agent would have to wait for five seconds to ensure the reservation for the corresponding investor's order was confirmed and the respective transaction was successfully approved. Such a time lag could be minimized by increasing the frequency of off-chain balance aggregation calling from the off-chain application. After testing with real-life workloads,

the system would have had to go through process iterations and performance fine-tuning to ensure that the solution capabilities were aligned with the business requirements and expectations.

Data privacy and cross-channel communication

Security and privacy of data are of critical importance to preserve the sensitive information of all participants in the blockchain network. There are several methods which can be implemented in Hyperledger Fabric

to ensure the data is safe, secure and available to everyone on need-to-know basis. In the solution prototype,

two mechanisms were used during the assessment.

Access Control Language (ACL)

Access Control Language (ACL), an authorization that provides declarative access control in Hyperledger Composer, is implemented to distinguish different forms of access by participants or organizations in the blockchain network by specifying resources to which they are granted access. In this assessment, data visibility for

all users was restricted with extra access control logic, implemented in smart contract's Access Control Lists. Users from selling agent organizations were able to see only the information related to them, whilst users from the registrar and CSD could view all the data in the ledger. The solution prototype with ACL demonstrated that it was able to control the rights of each user according to the operations that were defined
in the ACL file.

Channel

A private channel is a separate communication channel for sharing data with specific participants. Selling agents, for example, do not want to share their own details of sales transactions with other selling agents. Based on this requirement, a private channel was implemented to allow private data to be used and shared only with specifically defined participants. The remaining amount was shared between the selling agents so that they could access to an identical source for making bond reservations on a first-come, first-served basis. To enable this, the public channel, which recorded the remaining amount, was also implemented in the blockchain network for every selling agent to access. Figure 4.6 illustrates the concept as designed.

Thus, the number of communication channels required depended on the number of selling agents in the network. The total number of communication channels could be calculated from the number of selling agent organizations (n) that had a node plus one => (n) + 1 channels.

The result showed that participants could retrieve information in those specific channels for which they were authorized. According to the diagram, the registrar and CSD were registered for Chaincode 1, which was the public channel to provide the remaining amount for checking whether sufficient bonds were available for reservation. Chaincode 2, however, was used only by selling agent A, registrar and CSD, because it was a private channel. The same pattern also applied to Chaincode 3, where data were privately shared only between selling agent B, registrar and CSD.

In conclusion, the cross-channel communication and private channel using a blockchain ledger with a subset of network for each selling agent functioned properly. The information was retrievable on a need-to-know basis and shared only between authorized participants in the segregated network. This fact proved that Hyperledger Fabric provides the capabilities of information sharing with data privacy requirements.

Besides the use of channels, Hyperledger Fabric also provided other confidentiality mechanisms which were not explored in this project. For example, the use of a private data collection feature offers more granular level transaction privacy than channels. This feature allows sensitive data to be stored only in a database that is local to the designated party and distributed only between other parties that are relevant to the transaction. References to the private transactions (but not the actual data itself) are updated to the public ledger between peers in the network and serve as verifiable proof of updates. Future work will consider taking advantage of these features to further optimize the solution as appropriate.

Message notification on blockchain

To facilitate the ease of doing business, message notification was implemented to notify relevant participants when a certain task was complete or required action. The event mechanism of Hyperledger Composer was used to achieve this requirement. Events were emitted by the Hyperledger Fabric Peer and delivered by Composer REST server to the web-based application over Web-Sockets. The

assessment found that the publish-subscribe model provided a reliable channel for message transfer. Furthermore, the history of message notifications was stored in an off-chain database to allow participants to retrieve information when needed later.

Deployment options

Data security is one of the most critical issues in financial services. In many cases, there are strict regulatory compliance requirements to ensure that arrangement for solutions and data are established on-premise instead of via cloud. The solution prototype was also deployed on-premise, in addition to cloud, to ensure that it performed smoothly and could satisfy the assessment.

Running in an on-premise environment, the prototype was modified by making minor changes in the same scripts used on cloud to align it with the configuration in the data centre. In the current setup, Hyperledger Fabric required two communication ports to be opened per peer, which were accommodated by firewall rules. Although performance fine-tuning was still required, the solution prototype was successfully migrated from cloud to the on-premise environment and functioned as expected.

High availability

In this assessment, the impacts of shutting down certain components of Hyperledger Fabric, including endorsing and ordering peers and Hyperledger Fabric CA were investigated.

Endorsing peers

The environment for the assessment was set up as shown in figure 4.7. The registrar and CSD were endorsers and each of them consisted of two peers in "Channel A". In Hyperledger Fabric, an endorsement policy describes the conditions by which a transaction can be endorsed. A transaction can only be considered valid if it has been endorsed according to its policy.

In this example, we defined an endorsement policy whereby a minimum of three out of four peers would be the number of endorsing peers. To assess the lack of availability, each endorsing peer was shut down to investigate its consequence in the following scenarios. The assessment successfully demonstrated the availability of endorsing peers according to the endorsement policy.

Certificate Authority

The environment for assessing the availability of Hyperledger Fabric CA was identical to that for endorsing peers shown in figure 4.7. The registrar and CSD both had one Hyperledger Fabric CA and two peers. The assessment found that if one of two Hyperledger Fabric CA were available, certificate issuance could be performed. In addition, a transaction could proceed, even though both CAs were not available after a certificate had been issued. The result of scenarios is shown in the table below:

In summary, Hyperledger Fabric proved its capabilities to function properly when a subset of endorsing peers was available to endorse a transaction according to the endorsement policy. Transactions could be performed continuously, even if some of Hyperledger Fabric CAs, Kafkas, Zookeepers, and ordering peers were not available. Moreover, the data of failed peers could be synchronized in the channel once they were fully recovered. Besides SOLO and Kafka which is available out of the box, the ordering service is designed to be pluggable to support other implementation forms.

Performance

Government savings bonds can be sold via selling agents' branches, ATMs, mobile banking, and internet banking. Currently, four selling agents operate over 4,000 branches across Thailand. In the worst-case scenario,

an excessive number of transactions could be submitted through those sales channels at the same time and intensively during a period of high demand. Any solution, therefore, must be designed to be able to handle extreme conditions without compromising performance.

While the focus of the proof of concept was to address the functional requirements, several performance tests was executed against the requirements of the project. The tests were conducted over both a cloud and on-premise environment.

One of the experiments looked at the network topology. From the experiments, it was observed that the number of peers had a larger impact on performance, whilst other factors, such as the number of API instances and block-size configurations, did not significantly affect performance.

For the performance test conducted on-premises, the focus was on the infrastructure configurations that could enhance performance, such as storage types, number of Central Processing Units (CPUs) and memory capacity.

It was observed that the solution prototype developed using Go performed better by increasing the number of CPUs, as well as having greater memory size and changing the consensus algorithm to Kafka/Zookeeper. It was found that the performance was better than the SOLO consensus used for development and testing, as it could handle 1,000 concurrent transactions without rejecting any transactions.

As the performance results described here are specific to the nature of the project and setup, it does not aim to represent the performance potential of the underlying technology nor does it attempt to be exhaustive in its scope. Nevertheless, the exercise served as a useful reference on the performance characteristic of the solution and enables a better understanding of contributing factors that could have an impact on performance.

Summary of the DLT Bond Project

The DLT Scripless Bond project has proven that blockchain technology can drive the business transformation of government savings bonds. Its benefits and business values are shared across stakeholders, providing improved transparency, higher efficiencies and more effective management of information.

Blockchain technology also brings a shifting paradigm of ecosystem services and management. Preparations for establishing the appropriate governance, business and operating models for all stakeholders will be initiated to encourage the expansion of business networks and incorporate the emergence of new technologies and opportunities arising from them.

To bring about lasting value, the effective collaboration of related stakeholders is key. The contribution of all participants is highly valued and provides the industry with greater understanding of business processes in developing prototypes. BOT and market participants together recognize there is much work ahead,

in order to overcome the challenges of implementing a blockchain solution in the real world.

This proof of concept is just the first step that paves the way for the journey in developing Thailand's market infrastructure for government and corporate securities markets in the near future.

B) NATIONAL DIGITAL ID

Government identification systems are an important issue in the digital world. The government has adopted technology to serve the policy of Thailand 4.0. The national identity still segmented and distributed between government agencies, not holistically, which bring inconvenience to the users because each service must be registered and the users have to remember the username and password for every service. Thus results in bad practice of security when users use the same password.

Blockchain digital identity is now especially outstanding. The technologies still lacks the development of personal identification however access to traditional services like as a legal & political right, finance services, education, health services, social benefit or participant in the digital world like a web services, professional network, e-commerce, marketplace, social communities both need the identification function when they need to access services.

National Digital ID Blockchain Consortium was set up which is a secure and simple service that has the functionality of identification. The NIDBC framework consists of three part, which are smart contracts, libraries, and an application. The application keeps private keys. Smart contracts are the core of the identity services and incorporate logic. Libraries are integrated with third-party services. NIDBC identities have many variations for instance personality, devices, and entities. NIDBC identities are self- service, Implication for users are entirely operated and managed by themselves, and do not depend on centralized third parties for set permission or proof. A core function of NIDBC is that it can digitally sign and verify a claim, action, or transaction, which covers a wide range of application case studies. A digital ID stays cryptographically linked to off chain data. Every identity is able to store the hash of an attributed data, which secure the data corresponding with identity. The digital ID can update the file by themselves, for example, adding more information, and grant permission to read, write, and update specific files because the user can access the blockchain, NIDBC can control digital resources like cryptocurrencies or the other token.

National Digital ID based on the BC. Framework is composed of five phases, including Identity and Services Provider Registration Phase, User Privacy Creation Phase, User Registration Phase, User Authentication Phase and More Information Request Phase as the following:

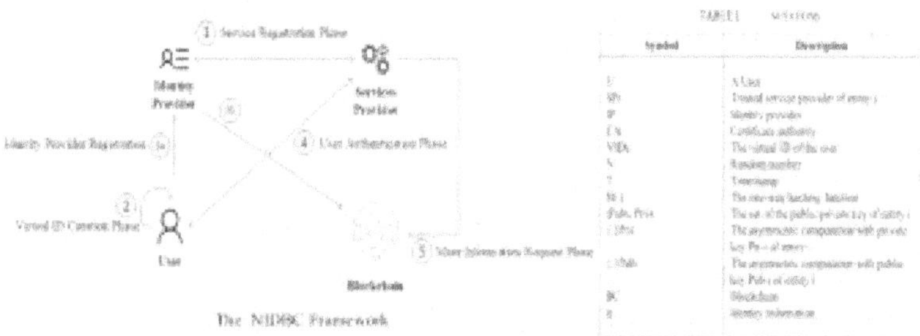

1.6: NIDBC: National ID on the Blockchain

i) Identity and Services Provider Registration Phase

In this phase, Both SP and IP need register in the system. All parties provide, exchange information, i.e., Service Information, IP address, and Permission to request certificates from CA. SP requests for membership to acquire identity information for U access services. In the same way, IP updates available information to SP whenever SP leaves the system. IP collects all the list of updated content to create catalog identity information. SP registers with IP by creating a message that includes their information along with signing their private keys and public keys. Then they send the message to IP, when IP receives the message, IP uses attached public key to decrypt the message, then IP validates SP and creates a new message stating whether it accepts or rejects. Then it sends it back through an SSL (Secure Socket Layer) communications channel to SP. After that, SP receives the message; SP uses their private keys to decrypt the message. SP sends their identity information message to IP along with the encrypted public key of SP and hashes content along with the signed private key of SP for message integrity and mutual trust sender. Whenever IP receives the message, IP will decrypt the message by using its private key to get the identity information and validates the sender by checking the owner of the private key and validates the hash value for message integrity.

ii) User Privacy Creation Phase

In this phase, U creates an asymmetric key of the private and the public key. U creates VIDu instead of using public identity to protect their privacy. Next, U keeps private key safely. Finally, U creates VIDu by utilizing the hash of public key so that the mechanism for generating the VIDu can be similar to the Bitcoin address.

iii) User Registration Phase

In this phase, U registers to the IP but is not registered with the SP. U needs to use a service offered by the SP, but U does not want the creation of a new ID and provides personal information to the SP for the service. U sends their information including the public key of U and VIDu to IP. After IP receives, IP creates their own digital signature. IP sends public key of U and VIDu that has been signed with SP's private key to BC. Then IP sends SP's public key to U.

iv) *User Authentication Phase*

In this phase, SP reads the user's VIDu and user's public key information from the BC, when the user requests to access the service to the VIDu. SP can confirm whether the claimed VIDu from the user is the one registered with the BC by accessing the BC. If the confirmation is correct, the partner begins the mutual authentication procedure for the user with the user's VIDu and user's public key obtained from the BC.

v) More Information Request Phase

SP wants more information of U, SP requests to IP for providing its service to U. For instance, if SP is National Health Security Office (NHSO), thus it requires at least the U medical treatment records to deliver claim. SP requests information from U.

C) DIGITAL CBDC

The Bank of Thailand (BOT) has announced the project to develop the prototype of the payment system for businesses using Central Bank Digital Currency (CBDC), which will build upon knowledge from Project Inthanon. The project scope will include conducting a feasibility study and developing a process to integrate CBDC with the business' innovative platform.

The BOT recognizes and supports the important roles of financial innovation and technology in enhancing the competitiveness and readiness of the business sector entering the digital age. The project marks an important step in broadening CBDC's scope and adoption to wider audiences, starting with large corporates. In this project, the CBDC prototype will be integrated with the procurement and financial management systems of the Siam Cement Public Company Limited and its suppliers developed by Digital Ventures Company Limited. The prototype is expected to serve as a financial innovation that enables higher payment efficiency for businesses such as increasing flexibility for fund transfers or delivering faster and more agile payments between suppliers. The project will begin in July 2020 and is expected to conclude by the end of the year, after which the BOT will publish the project summary and outcome accordingly.

In addition, Project Inthanon, the collaborative project between the BOT and the eight leading financial institutions to study and develop the proof-of-concept for domestic wholesale funds transfer using wholesale CBDC, has been accomplished in January 2020 with the successful completion of the cross-border transfer prototype co-developed with the Hong Kong Monetary Authority (HKMA). In the next step, the BOT, the HKMA and the participating financial institutions will continue to collaborate and experiment CBDC for other use cases in cross-

The BOT strongly believes that continuous collaborations and development in financial innovation with the business sector would lay foundation in building technological capacity and readiness for the financial services and businesses rapidly entering the digital age. Moreover, the BOT remains open to private sector engagements to further promote innovation and explore potential uses cases for future adoptions.

Project Inthanon is a collaborative effort with the goal to develop and test a proof-of-concept (POC) for domestic wholesale fund transfer using wholesale Central Bank Digital Currency (wholesale CBDC). The project explores the potential in using Distributed Ledger Technology (DLT) to enhance Thailand's financial infrastructure and to encourage collaborative learning among involved parties.

Project Inthanon Phase I (August 2018 – January 2019) was conducted by the BOT, a technology partner R3, and eight participating banks including Bangkok Bank Public Company Limited, Krung Thai Bank Public Company Limited, Bank of Ayudhya Public Company Limited, Kasikornbank Public Company Limited, Siam Commercial Bank Public Company Limited, Thanachart Bank Public Company Limited, Standard Chartered Bank (Thai) Public Company Limited, and The Hongkong and Shanghai Banking Corporation Limited.

The outcome and findings of Project Inthanon Phase I

The results of Project Inthanon Phase I indicated

that DLT can fulfil basic payment functionalities. In addition, the technology demonstrated capabilities to help enhance payment efficiency and to support interbank transfer and settlement during off-hours. It is worth noting that despite its high capabilities, DLT would need more time to mature to the stage in which the technology can be fully adopted for the payment system infrastructure. More experiments would be needed to further affirm DLT's capabilities, and any challenges to comply with international payments standard such as scalability, security and system resiliency should be explored.

The learning outcome and test results from Phase I provide an important basis for the development of Thailand's payment system. (Further details on the Phase I results are available for download at the following URL: https://www.bot.or.th/English/FinancialMarkets/ProjectInthanon/Documents/Inthanon_Phase1_Report.pdf

The Scope of Project Inthanon Phase II

Based on the developed POC, the BOT, R3 and the eight participating banks will continue to collaboratively explore further applications of DLT in two areas: (1) Interbank Trading and Repurchase transaction to reduce delivery and settlement time for financial transactions related to BOT issued debt instruments on DLT system, and (2) Regulatory Compliance and Data Reconciliation to explore how DLT can facilitate banks' reconciliation of customer accounts and money transfers in compliance with the BOT regulations in order to reduce error and associated compliance costs.

Project Inthanon Phase II will start in February 2019 and is expected to be completed by the third quarter of 2019 after which the BOT will publish a project report accordingly.

SCG has announced that it has signed a memorandum of understanding (MoU) with the Bank of Thailand and Digital Ventures to develop a prototype system of Central Bank Digital Currency (CBDC) to enhance the efficiency of purchasing and payment management in the business sector. The CBDC is being developed to reduce transaction steps and processing time, which will be conducive to boosting business confidence and competitiveness and promoting Fintech innovation in the future.

3. NEXT NATION SCALE BLOCKCHAIN PROJECTS TO BE IMPLEMENTED

Smart Financial Infrastructure

The Smart Financial Infrastructure is made up of following 4 parts shown in the diagram, namely Payment mediators, Banking participants, Trade & Regulators.

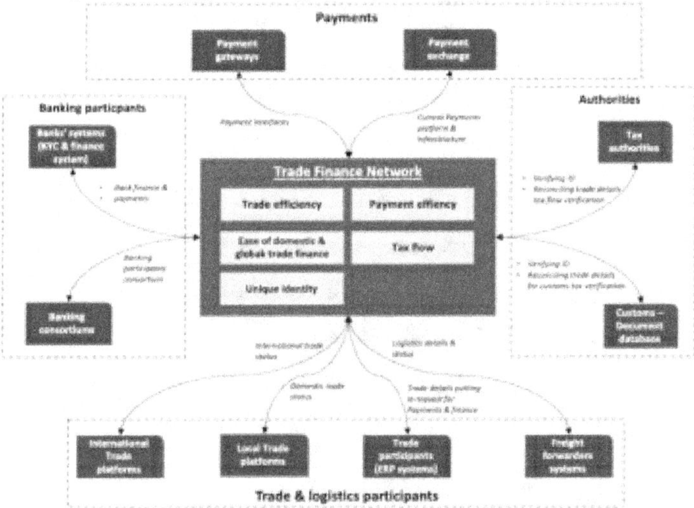

1.7: Thailand's Smart Financial Infrastructure over the Blockchain

Step 1 of the Smart Financial Infrastructure is Set up of Unique Trade Identity.

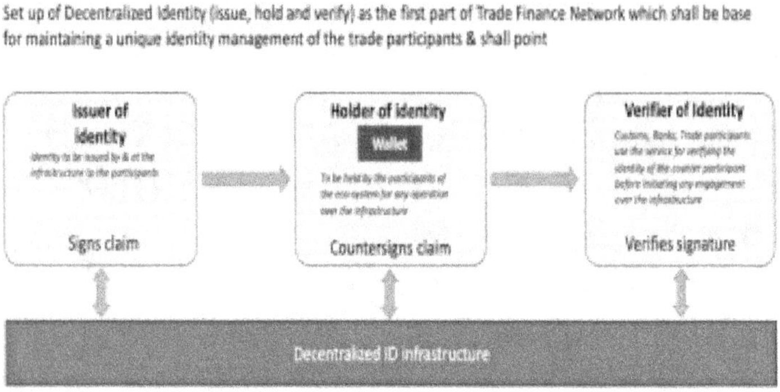

1.8: Decentralised Trader identity

Step 2: Set up of Network to capture Trade

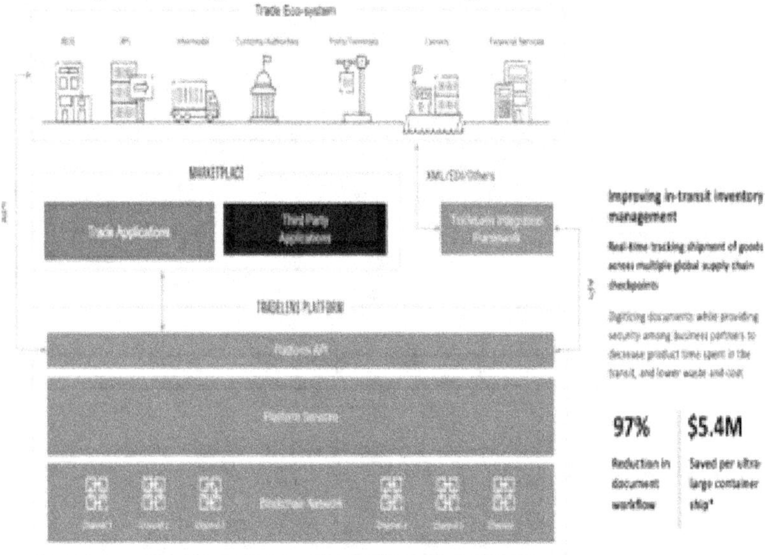

Step 2: Capture Trade details on Blockchain (Reference TradeLens Platform)

Step 3: Streamlining the payments and trade seamlessly across the financial network by integrating Blockchain platform with traditional payment gateways by getting the best of both.

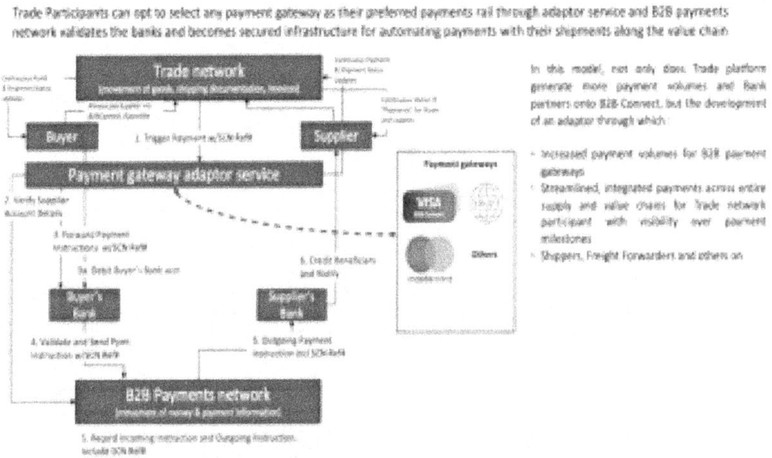

Step 3: Seamless financial Transactions across the Blockchain networks

Step 4: Set up of Domestic Finance network.

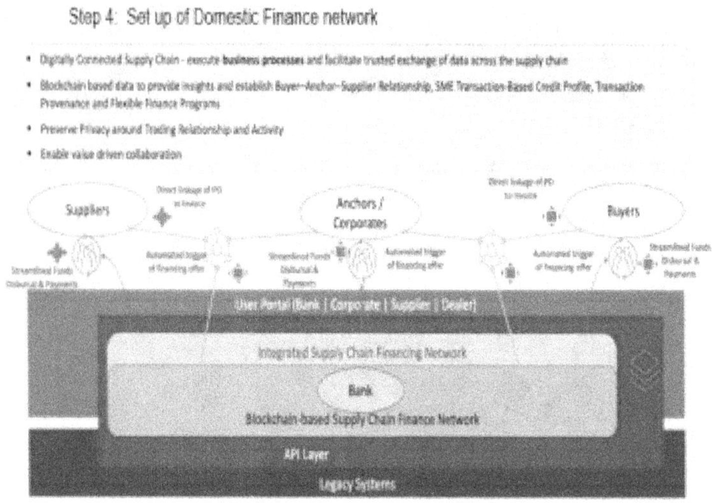

Step 4: Completing the Loop and facilitating

Supply Chain Finance by leveraging Blockchain

In this chapter, we have seen how a determined nation, strategically leverages Blockchain technology to turn around its financial system into a robust performance facilitator for boosting its trade and cutting down the costs of operation across various domains. This is the way to go for every country if they are not to be left behind as economically inefficient and poor performing countries unable to compete in the global markets. Thus, Blockchain is acting as a potentially powerful tool in re-defining the world financial order!

ABOUT THE AUTHOR

Srinivas Mahankali is an alumnus of IIT Madras and IIM Bangalore and has served as Head of Blockchain & Emerging Centres of Excellence in Government and Private Organisations. He is certified in Lean Six Sigma, NCFM Level 2, Capital Markets and R3 Corda & IBM Microservices and Digital Marketing.

He also led Strategy & IT for 3 years at Apollo LogiSolutions (ALS), India's leading integrated logistics services company. Here, he formulated & implemented the ABEX (Apollo Business Excellence) program, and executed a comprehensive overhaul of IT hardware, networking and ERP management at ALS. During his tenure as CIO, ALS won the awards, 'The Best Integrated Logistics Services Company' & Best Logistics CEO in India' in 2017.

While he has authored and co-authored two prominent books 'Blockchain–The Untold Story' and 'AI & ML Powered Agents of Automation and Successful Organisations in Action', respectively, his book 'Blockchain–The Untold Story' is the first ever book to be translated from English into Chinese by Artificial Engineering Bots.

Digital technologies have seen a massive adoption thanks to the Covid Pandemic . Governments across the world are adoption Blockchain to dramatically improve Governance. We take a look at simple approach to understand Blockchain applications in real life.

Srinivas Mahankali is an IIT and IIM alumnus & is pursuing his Global Doctorate in AI & Data Science at Rennes School of Business & INSOFE and DBA from SP Jain Global School of Management. As the inaugural Program Director of India' first University certified Post Grad Progtam in Blockchain by Amity University, he has mentored a number of Blockchain students across the world .He authored over 10 books in Technology and Management.

www.ingramcontent.com/pod-product-compliance
Lightning Source LLC
Chambersburg PA
CBHW060826220526
45466CB00003B/998
9798577667979